HowExpert

How To Make Hemp Jewelry

Your Step By Step Guide To Making Hemp Jewelry

HowExpert with Tabitha Chandler

Copyright HowExpert™
www.HowExpert.com

For more tips related to this topic, visit HowExpert.com/hempjewelry.

Recommended Resources

- HowExpert.com – Quick 'How To' Guides on All Topics from A to Z by Everyday Experts.
- HowExpert.com/free – Free HowExpert Email Newsletter.
- HowExpert.com/books – HowExpert Books
- HowExpert.com/courses – HowExpert Courses
- HowExpert.com/clothing – HowExpert Clothing
- HowExpert.com/membership – HowExpert Membership Site
- HowExpert.com/affiliates – HowExpert Affiliate Program
- HowExpert.com/writers – Write About Your #1 Passion/Knowledge/Expertise & Become a HowExpert Author.
- HowExpert.com/resources – Additional HowExpert Recommended Resources
- YouTube.com/HowExpert – Subscribe to HowExpert YouTube.
- Instagram.com/HowExpert – Follow HowExpert on Instagram.
- Facebook.com/HowExpert – Follow HowExpert on Facebook.

COPYRIGHT, LEGAL NOTICE AND DISCLAIMER:

COPYRIGHT © BY HOWEXPERT™ (OWNED BY HOT METHODS). ALL RIGHTS RESERVED WORLDWIDE. NO PART OF THIS PUBLICATION MAY BE REPRODUCED IN ANY FORM OR BY ANY MEANS, INCLUDING SCANNING, PHOTOCOPYING, OR OTHERWISE WITHOUT PRIOR WRITTEN PERMISSION OF THE COPYRIGHT HOLDER.

DISCLAIMER AND TERMS OF USE: PLEASE NOTE THAT MUCH OF THIS PUBLICATION IS BASED ON PERSONAL EXPERIENCE AND ANECDOTAL EVIDENCE. ALTHOUGH THE AUTHOR AND PUBLISHER HAVE MADE EVERY REASONABLE ATTEMPT TO ACHIEVE COMPLETE ACCURACY OF THE CONTENT IN THIS GUIDE, THEY ASSUME NO RESPONSIBILITY FOR ERRORS OR OMISSIONS. ALSO, YOU SHOULD USE THIS INFORMATION AS YOU SEE FIT, AND AT YOUR OWN RISK. YOUR PARTICULAR SITUATION MAY NOT BE EXACTLY SUITED TO THE EXAMPLES ILLUSTRATED HERE; IN FACT, IT'S LIKELY THAT THEY WON'T BE THE SAME, AND YOU SHOULD ADJUST YOUR USE OF THE INFORMATION AND RECOMMENDATIONS ACCORDINGLY.

THE AUTHOR AND PUBLISHER DO NOT WARRANT THE PERFORMANCE, EFFECTIVENESS OR APPLICABILITY OF ANY SITES LISTED OR LINKED TO IN THIS BOOK. ALL LINKS ARE FOR INFORMATION PURPOSES ONLY AND ARE NOT WARRANTED FOR CONTENT, ACCURACY OR ANY OTHER IMPLIED OR EXPLICIT PURPOSE.

ANY TRADEMARKS, SERVICE MARKS, PRODUCT NAMES OR NAMED FEATURES ARE ASSUMED TO BE THE PROPERTY OF THEIR RESPECTIVE OWNERS, AND ARE USED ONLY FOR REFERENCE. THERE IS NO IMPLIED ENDORSEMENT IF WE USE ONE OF THESE TERMS.

NO PART OF THIS BOOK MAY BE REPRODUCED, STORED IN A RETRIEVAL SYSTEM, OR TRANSMITTED BY ANY OTHER MEANS: ELECTRONIC, MECHANICAL, PHOTOCOPYING, RECORDING, OR OTHERWISE, WITHOUT THE PRIOR WRITTEN PERMISSION OF THE AUTHOR.

ANY VIOLATION BY STEALING THIS BOOK OR DOWNLOADING OR SHARING IT ILLEGALLY WILL BE PROSECUTED BY LAWYERS TO THE FULLEST EXTENT. THIS PUBLICATION IS PROTECTED UNDER THE US COPYRIGHT ACT OF 1976 AND ALL OTHER APPLICABLE INTERNATIONAL, FEDERAL, STATE AND LOCAL LAWS AND ALL RIGHTS ARE RESERVED, INCLUDING RESALE RIGHTS: YOU ARE NOT ALLOWED TO GIVE OR SELL THIS GUIDE TO ANYONE ELSE.

THIS PUBLICATION IS DESIGNED TO PROVIDE ACCURATE AND AUTHORITATIVE INFORMATION WITH REGARD TO THE SUBJECT MATTER COVERED. IT IS SOLD WITH THE UNDERSTANDING THAT THE AUTHORS AND PUBLISHERS ARE NOT ENGAGED IN RENDERING LEGAL, FINANCIAL, OR OTHER PROFESSIONAL ADVICE. LAWS AND PRACTICES OFTEN VARY FROM STATE TO STATE AND IF LEGAL OR OTHER EXPERT ASSISTANCE IS REQUIRED, THE SERVICES OF A PROFESSIONAL SHOULD BE SOUGHT. THE AUTHORS AND PUBLISHER SPECIFICALLY DISCLAIM ANY LIABILITY THAT IS INCURRED FROM THE USE OR APPLICATION OF THE CONTENTS OF THIS BOOK.

COPYRIGHT BY HOWEXPERT™ (OWNED BY HOT METHODS)
ALL RIGHTS RESERVED WORLDWIDE.

Table Contents

Recommended Resources 2
Introduction 6
   History 7
Chapter 1: A Few Things You Will Need 10
   Tools That Will Make Your Life Easier 11
      Bead Reamer 12
      Clasps 13
      Duct Tape 14
   Choosing Your Hemp 14
      Thick Hemp Versus Thin Hemp 15
   Waxed Hemp Versus Un-Waxed Hemp 16
   Dying Your Hemp 17
   Choosing Your Beads 18
   Protecting Your Hands 20
   Chapter Review: 20
Chapter 2: Things You Need To Know 22
   Making Your Loop: The Starting Point of Your Jewelry 23
   Tying the Knot 28
   Learning the Half Twist Knot 29
   Learning the Square Knot 35
   Learning the Half Hitch Knot 42
   Learning the Alternating Half Hitch Knot 45
   Learning the Overhand Knot 49
   Using What You Have Learned 52
   Chapter Review 52
Chapter 3: The Half Twist 54
   Alternating Half Twist Anklet 54
      Simple Half Twist Bracelet With Beads 65
   Examples of The Square Knot 69
      The Fishbone 69
      Choker With Square Knot Variation 76
      Square Knot Beaded Anklet 79
   The Half Hitch 85
      The Bar 85
   The Overhand Knot 90
      Overhand Knot Belt 90
   Chapter Review: 96
Chapter 4: How to Braid 97
   Braiding 97
   How to Weave 101

  Five Strand Woven Band Bracelet 101
  Seven Strand Woven Band Bracelet 105
 Chapter Review 110
Chapter 5: Mix It Up 112
 Pendant Jewelry 112
 Simple Overhand Knot Pendant Necklace 112
 Simple Overhand Knot Pendant Necklace Variation With Beads
 119
 Alternating Half Hitch Pendant Necklace 125
 Ways That You Can Make Your Jewelry Adjustable 128
  Braid Closure 128
  Square Knot Closure 131
  Single Bead Closure 136
  The Butterfly Knot 139
  2nd Single Bead Closure 142
  Multiple Knot Closure 143
  Multiple Bead Closure 143
 Chapter Review 144
A Note from the Author 145
 About the Expert 147
Recommended Resources 148

Introduction

I have fond memories of going to Grateful Dead concerts as a teenager. I was twelve when their lead guitarist Jerry died, but fortunately the rest of the band continued to tour. The lot scenes at the concerts were incredible, especially the spontaneous drum circles that seemed to erupt on every corner. It was a sea of tie dye and corduroy patchwork, both of which I am in love with. Not to mention the fairy wings, bubbles and balloons. The air was sweet with the scent of incense, patchouli, and, well, other things. It was magical, like a scene from what I could only have imagined Woodstock had been. I was amazed by the people. Everyone seemed so friendly and full of hugs, and no one acted like a stranger.

Vendors flooded the lots outside the concerts. Some of them sold food, but most of them sold art of one kind or another. Among the artists were glassblowers, clothing makers, jewelry makers and everything in between. You name it and you could find it, or if you couldn't, someone knew someone who could. I met one artist who was set up in the back of her highly decorated Volkswagon bus. On display was every color and style of hemp jewelry that I could ever have imagined. She even made toe rings from hemp! I was completely blown away. I mean, I always had a thing for macramé, but this stuff was unbelievable! I almost didn't want to touch it, for fear that I would somehow contaminate it with my untrained hands. I never saw the jewelry maker after that, but I have never forgotten the impression that her jewelry made on me. That was the moment I knew that I had to learn the art of macramé for myself.

My first attempt at making jewelry was terrible. I bought a jewelry kit from a large chain store expecting to make a masterpiece on my first try. It was one that had precut hemp strands and all of the beads and such that were necessary to make a necklace. The instructions that came with it were—let's just say "less than clear" to be nice. The illustrations were even worse than the instructions. By the end of my attempt, I had a string of knotty ugliness that resembled a new dreadlock. If you have never seen a new dreadlock, think of an angry or frightened cat's tail. I thought I had followed the instructions exactly as they were written. Maybe I am just a little terrible at following instructions. Either way, it would be a while before I would try it again. A couple of years, actually, until I re-united with a friend (now best friend), Stephanie- aka Moonshyne. She showed me the knots and I couldn't believe how simple it actually was. Once again I cursed the unclear directions I'd followed in the past, and myself for giving up so easily.

Moonshyne and I began making a lot of jewelry together after that, and many times we would even make our own beads and pendants for the jewelry. Getting the basics down opened the door to a whole new world of jewelry making for me. I began experimenting with new knots, colors, styles, and sizes of hemp. I have not turned back or stopped experimenting to this day, and I still have a lot to learn. Ultimately, I have gained a new respect for crafting and art.

That brings me to the point of this guide. With the right instruction, hemp jewelry making can be very simple. My hope is that this book caters to everyone, including people like me who just do not get anything out of looking at a couple of drawings. Is it just me, or is it difficult to follow squiggly lines with arrows going in four different directions? In my opinion, if you do not have someone to show you how to do something in person, step by step pictures are the next best thing.

History

Macramé: (*n*) a type of ornamental work made by knotting and weaving coarse thread into a pattern [via the French and Italians from Turkish *makrama* towel, and/or from Arabic *migramah* striped cloth]

There is some argument as to the origin of the word macramé. Some say that is derived from the Turkish word *makrama*, while others believe it is from the Arabic word *migramah*. The general consensus, however, seems to be that the art of macramé has its roots in Arabic tradition. It is thought to have originated sometime in the thirteenth century. Early accounts of macramé include carvings and statues that show materials and clothing adorned with macramé knotting.

The art first spread to Spain and then was picked up by sailors who made macramé items to trade as they reached land. In the fourteenth and fifteenth centuries, macramé found its way to Italy and France, where it was widely practiced and picked up by more sailors. Thus, the art was spread throughout the world as sailors moved from coast to coast, eventually reaching North America from Europe sometime in the seventeenth century.

In the 1960s and 1970s, macramé became very popular in both the United Kingdom and the United States of America. It was seen in home décor as well as jewelry, ranging from plant hangers and even furniture, to earrings, bracelets, and other jewelry. Its popularity waned for a while, and the art became more widely, but wrongly, attributed to the hippie movement. It is now making a comeback in jewelry, clothing, and even in the form of sculpture. Phew! Now this is great news for a hippie like me....

Hemp: *(n)* -the tough, coarse fiber of the cannabis plant, used to make cordage

Hemp is harvested from the *Cannabis sativa* L. plant. Though it is a member of the Cannabis family, it lacks the high concentration of THC that is found in some of the other Cannabis plants. THC is the chemical in marijuana (harvested from other plants in the Cannabis family) that causes a high, or altered state of mind. This plant family has been used for thousands of years in many different cultures. There is evidence of its cultivation as far back as 8000 B.C. Throughout ancient Europe, Africa and Asia, hemp was used as food, medicine, clothing and for other fibers such as paper. The trend spread throughout the west and into the United States. In the 1600s hemp was considered to be legal tender in the United States, and there were even mandates put in place for growing crops of hemp. As a matter of fact, in the 1700s farmers in certain states who did not grow hemp could be jailed. Washington himself grew hemp on his own plantation. Another interesting tidbit: Lincoln used the oil from the seeds to burn in his lamps. During the last century, however, the practice of cultivating hemp in the States has been largely banned. Locally grown hemp did regain its legal status for a short while during WWII when the normal supply line was cut off. The American military needed the fiber to produce rope, webbing and other such things badly needed by soldiers. After the war, unfortunately, hemp did not retain its legal status. Prohibition had become widespread throughout the world due to the narcotic properties of the female cannabis plant. The cannabis plant family has certainly gained a terrible reputation through the years, but arguably it has made quite a contribution to countless civilizations. This guide serves to show yet another contribution; one I take great pleasure in sharing.

Chapter 1: A Few Things You Will Need

Firstly, you will need patience- and a lot of it. Do not expect to get it perfect the first time. Maybe not even the second. But, with a little practice, the knots and techniques presented in this guide will become second nature to you.

Second, you will need time. Making hemp jewelry can be a bit time consuming while you are learning. Taking the time to learn and practice, though, is highly fulfilling.

Very few materials are needed to make hemp jewelry. A few strands (or a ball) of hemp, scissors, and some beads (optional) are the only major requirements. Hemp is easy to find. It can be purchased at almost any craft store or online retailer. If you are purchasing large quantities of it, online shopping usually tends to be cheaper. Though, one ball of hemp (somewhere between $5-$10) makes several long necklaces. So if you are not making jewelry to sell, it is usually not necessary to go out and purchase hemp in large quantities.

One thing I keep handy at all times is fabric glue. I always recommend using fabric glue to secure knots at the end of necklaces. It is not a necessity, so if you do not have it handy, do not let it stop you from making jewelry. However, the next time you are out and about, you may want to pick some up. Make sure that it is clear drying, for obvious reasons. You can find fabric glue in pretty much any craft or chain store. It is usually with the sewing materials.

Tools That Will Make Your Life Easier

As I said before, all you really need is scissors, hemp, and maybe some beads to make jewelry. Having some tools on hand, though, can save you a lot of time and hassle. Here are a few things that might come in handy:

Bead Reamer

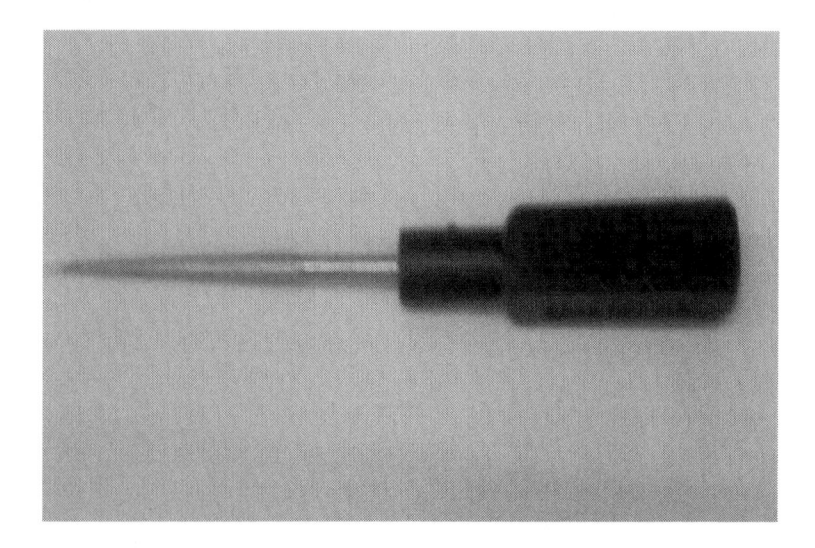

A lot of the time, especially when you purchase beads in bulk, you will find beads with obstructed or irregularly sized holes. You can use the bead reamer to remove obstructions or to make the holes in the beads larger to fit your hemp. This tool works best with wooden and plastic beads. It can be used, with caution, on clay and fimo beads. I would not, however, recommend its use for glass or stone beads.

The picture above shows some pretty common obstructions that I have run into while making jewelry. These have been especially common in wooden beads, but they are easy to remove. Even higher quality or more expensive beads are going to have some imperfections. It is just something that has to be dealt with, a fact of life, so to say. So it is best to be prepared for such things. In times when I did not have a bead reamer handy, I have been known to scrape away these imperfections with scissors, a knife, or whatever was nearby. Be careful with the scissors and knives, though. I hope I do not need to express why. From the nicks and cuts I have gotten, maybe someone should have expressed such to me.....

Clasps

Clasps can be used to make your jewelry look more professional. You can also use them to make your jewelry adjustable. I have never really used clasps in my jewelry, but they are an option and a must for many. I am of the opinion that clasps give a more store-bought appearance. I like for my jewelry to retain its handmade and rustic charm.

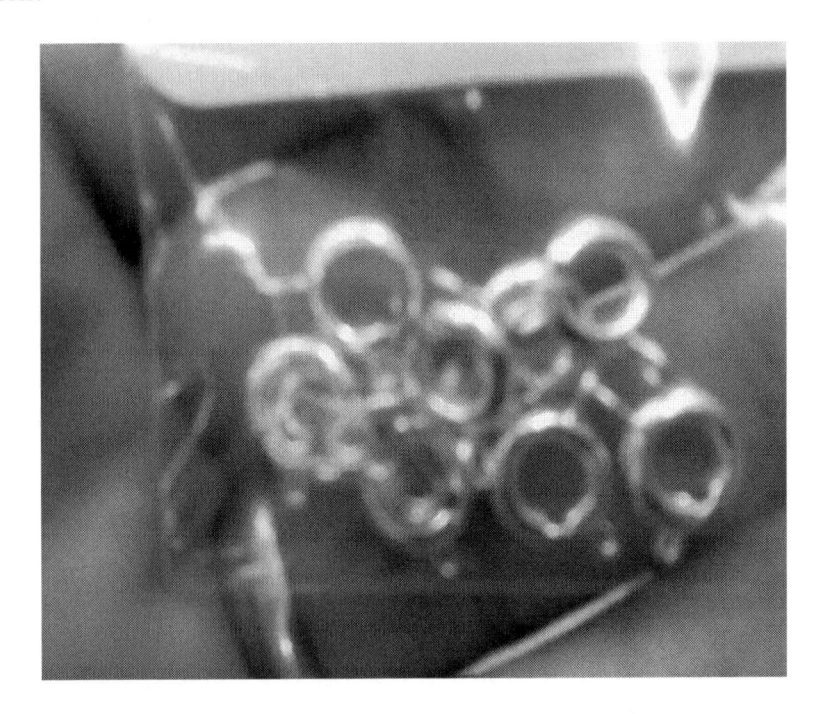

Duct Tape

If you can't duct it, um, forget it. Isn't that how the saying goes? Duct tape comes in handy with those pesky strands that need to stay still, especially the middle strands that you are tying knots around. If you do not have a board and a couple of nails handy, just duct tape the ends of your strands to any surface. It works in a pinch. You may even find it preferable.

Choosing Your Hemp

The picture below shows a ball of thin hemp. Also known as 2mm or 20 lb. hemp.

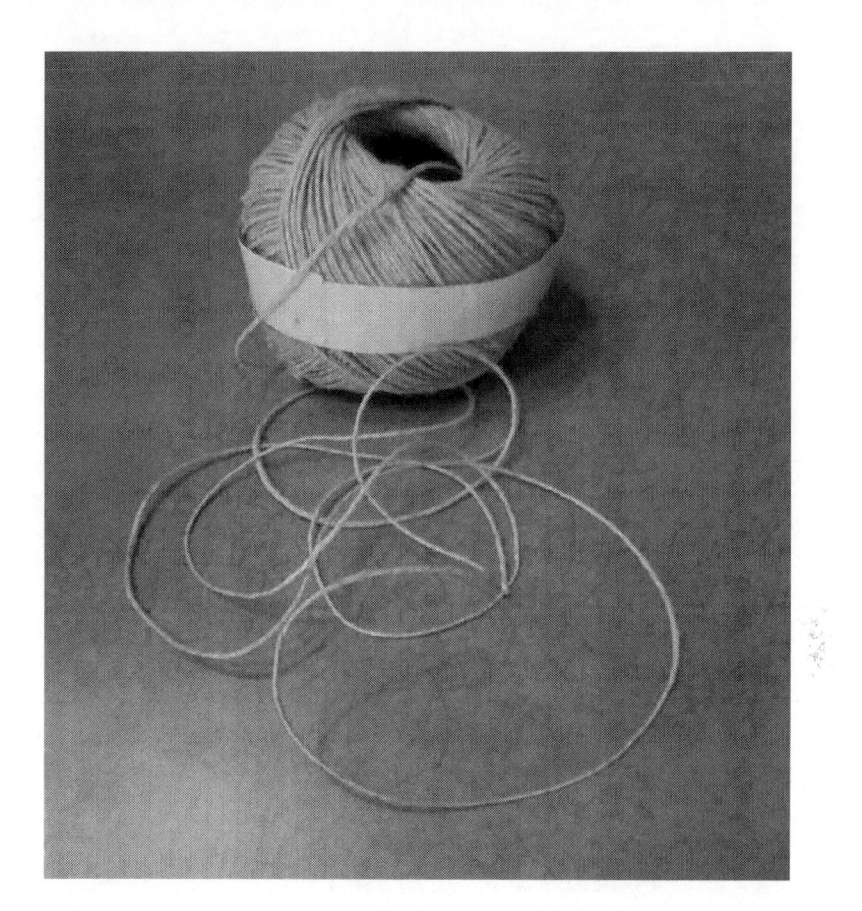

Thick Hemp Versus Thin Hemp

With so many types of hemp to choose from, where do you start? That is all a matter of preference. For me, it was easier to start with thinner hemp strands. It was easier to grasp the thin hemp and easier to pull my knots tight. The thinner hemp tends to have fewer uneven spots and slightly less fraying as well, or at least it is less noticeable. So you are not quite as likely to run into trouble spots with knotting or beads. Using thinner hemp also makes finding beads easier, since most chain stores carry a wider variety of smaller beads than larger beads.

Thicker strands do have their advantages, though. For one, it is easier to see the knots you are forming and to keep count of the knots. When adding beads to your jewelry, keeping count of the knots is very important so that you have symmetry. Otherwise, you will end up with a lop-sided piece that will not wear very well. One thing to note: The thicker your hemp is, the more length you will need for your jewelry. The thicker hemp will make much larger knots, using up more strand as you work.

Waxed Hemp Versus Un-Waxed Hemp

For most of my jewelry, I like to use natural un-waxed hemp (with the exception of when I'm tying a Fishbone knot, but more on that later). Again, this is just a matter of preference. I like the look of natural hemp and do not usually mind the occasional frayed spot or a little unevenness in the thickness of the hemp. One very slight drawback to using natural hemp is that your jewelry may seem a little stiff and scratchy on your skin at first. Not to worry, the natural oils in your skin will quickly soften the hemp. If you wear the jewelry while bathing or get it wet a couple times, it will soften even faster.

One advantage to using natural hemp is that it can be dyed before use. Dying, for me, has proven to be time consuming and a lot of work, but worthwhile when I cannot find pre-dyed hemp in the color I need.

If you want your jewelry to have a cleaner look, (i.e. no frayed strands) you may want to use waxed hemp. The waxed hemp also has the benefit of more uniform thickness, so you will not have to fight to get a bead over the occasional lump in your strand. A disadvantage, though, is that if you have to back up and undo a couple of knots, it is much more difficult because waxed hemp sort of sticks to itself. I am not particularly fond of the waxed stuff because I do not like the sticky feeling on my hands. It reminds me a little of getting glue from a glue stick on my skin, though I don't notice it so much during wear. The waxed stuff is also a bit softer when first crafted.

Dying Your Hemp

A lot of beautiful jewelry can be made with natural, undyed hemp, but dying opens up a lot of creative possibilities, as well as pre-softens your hemp. Again, this only works with natural hemp. Waxed hemp will not evenly absorb the color, if any color is absorbed at all. Start with a large bowl or basin, depending on how much hemp you want to dye. Mix the dye according to the directions on the package. With most dyes, vinegar can be added to, or used instead of water for a brighter shade of color. A lot of times the package will specify how much vinegar to use. If the package does not say, you can always call the company's customer service line to be sure before using any vinegar.

It is always a good idea to lay a protective cover over your work area before you start. You may even want to do your dying outside to avoid the possibility of permanently staining your floor or countertops. Always, always wear latex gloves as the dye will also color your skin, and the color is not easily washed out. Think back to how gorgeous your hands were the last time you dyed Easter eggs. Soak your hemp in the dye mixture for at least an hour. Rinse thoroughly and allow the hemp to dry. It is very important that you rinse well, otherwise the color may bleed onto your clothing or skin after you have made your jewelry. You may need to repeat the process once or twice, depending on how dark or bright of a shade you want. So wait until your hemp dries before you throw out your dye mixture, as you may want to re-use it.

It does take quite a while for the hemp to dry, so be prepared to wait. Some of my best results have been with sun drying. In the winter, however, sun drying may not be an option. As an alternative, you can throw up a clothesline type setup over the bathtub and hang your hemp there. I have done so with some rope, string, and even hemp held by a couple of thumbtacks with good results. Hang your hemp and let dry. This works best if you have a fan blowing on the hemp, but it will still take a while to dry. If you only have one bathroom, this method could be a problem. Another option is to use a clothes dryer. Use a low heat setting for drying your hemp. Be aware, though, if you decide to go this route you will have to clean your dryer very well before drying any clothing. You will also have to spend a good amount of time untangling your hemp. If you do not own a clothes dryer and can't dry your hemp over the bath tub, you could use a hair dryer to speed the drying process a little. It will still, however, be time consuming.

Choosing Your Beads

I always find myself lost in the bead isle of any craft store. It is one place I have to really discipline myself with money, otherwise I would walk out with a bag full of beads and no paycheck. (Yes, my bead addiction is that bad). All of the beads look so glittery and pretty on the shelf, and I love glittery things. But the beads might not look quite so glittery and pretty once I get them home. Especially in lieu of a paycheck. So I have to go into the craft store already having an idea of what I want. I may not know exactly, but I have a plan for color, shape, and size at the very least.

It is always better to overestimate the size of your beads than to underestimate. This is because of the sometimes uneven thickness of hemp. For good measure, I usually take a few strands of the hemp I will be using when I choose my beads. I make sure that the beads do not fit snugly on the strands, so that I can avoid the problem of being halfway through a piece and then having to start over because the beads will no longer fit. (I learned this the hard way, though in most cases I can push through using a bead reamer). When using natural hemp, having a stock of wooden beads always comes in handy. I usually buy these in bulk because they come in so many different colors, styles, and shapes and are so versatile as filler beads. Because one package of wooden beads contains so many different sizes, I also have the choice to use different sizes of hemp. Plus, wood materials are much more environmentally friendly than the plastic stuff, as long as they are harvested responsibly. I have a thing for natural products. For me, nothing beats earth tones, natural hemp, and natural looking or hand carved wood beads.

If you plan to sell the jewelry you make, keep the cost of the beads in mind. Remember that the more the beads cost, the more you will have to charge for your jewelry. So think cheap or bulk for the most part, but do not sacrifice quality. You do not have to spend a lot of money to make great jewelry. Being able to keep your prices reasonable will help you sell more jewelry to a larger variety of people. Save the more expensive stuff for when you have made a little money, or to sell to a smaller group of people who want specialty items.

Protecting Your Hands

Hemp jewelry making can be pretty harsh on your hands. You want to monitor your fingers as you work. When I first started making hemp jewelry, I ended up with a lot of blisters on my fingers. As I pulled my knots tight, the hemp would rub against my skin. Much of the time I did not notice until my fingers started to itch and hurt, because I was so engaged in what I was doing and because the rubbing was so subtle. At that point I already had little raw spots on my fingers, a bit like carpet burn. Eventually my skin got used to it, and now I do not have a problem with burns. When out of practice for a little while, though, I have found that wearing band aids or medical tape on my fingers helps keep them from getting rubbed and blistered. Duct tape will work just as well if it is all you have nearby.

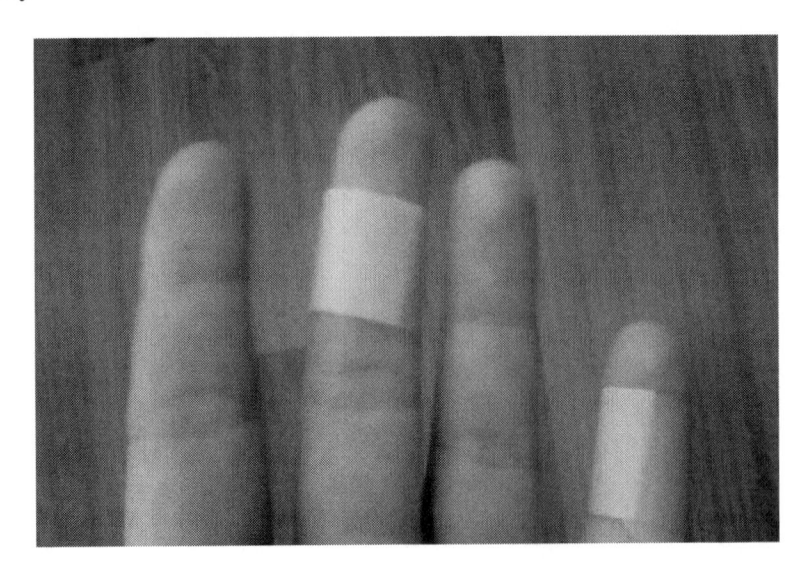

Chapter Review:

- All you really need to make wonderful jewelry is hemp and scissors, and maybe a few beads.
- Fabric glue is recommended throughout this guide. It is not a necessity, but I strongly recommend it to keep your end knots stronger and less likely to unravel.

- Having tools on hand, such as a bead reamer and duct tape, will save a lot of time as you make your jewelry.
- If you can't find the color of hemp you desire, dye it!
- Choose your beads carefully. Think size, price, and versatility. Try to take a sample of the hemp you will be using with you when you are bead hunting. If you can't, remember that it's always better to get them a little larger than you need than to wind up with beads that are too small to work with.
- Be mindful of your hands. The constant pulling and tugging on hemp can leave you with blisters. Use band aids or medical tape on your fingers if this becomes a problem.

Chapter 2: Things You Need To Know

First and foremost, decide the length your piece needs to be. Keep in mind that the thicker your hemp is, the longer the strands you will need. In general you will need strands that are about five to six times the length of what you would like your jewelry to be, and then at least one more length for good measure (as you will be folding the strands in half). The reason for the extra span is that you will need much longer strands than the actual length of the jewelry you are making. Knotting uses up the strands very quickly. It is always better to have more than you need. You can always subtract, but you cannot add. For a lot of hemp jewelry, all of your strands can be equal in length. However, in some cases, such as weaving, you will need a strand or strands that are longer than the rest. I will go into more detail on that later.

A note about the measurements in this guide: I have never been one to really measure anything. I tend to eyeball ingredients when I cook. And, I admit, I have had to return a couple of sets of curtains and blinds in my day because I did not bother to measure the windows before purchasing them. As for hemp jewelry, I have never taken a measurement for anything I have made. I learned as I went that for a choker I might need three arm spans, or for a bracelet I might need two. Sometimes, I pulled out way too much hemp, and other times I came up short. It's a process that is worth going through, in my humble opinion.

In this guide I will refer to "your desired length" on several occasions. What I mean is the length you prefer your finished product to be, not the length of the strands you will need to make the jewelry.

You can always save leftover or scrap strands to make key chains, earrings, or even to practice a new knot before making jewelry. If you have kids the scraps are great for arts and crafts time. My ten year old son has a lot of fun making "noodle" pictures with my leftovers. Who knew a little glue, paper, and string could be so awesome?

Making Your Loop: The Starting Point of Your Jewelry

To begin most pieces of jewelry you will need to tie a loop. Regardless of how many strands you are using, the loop is tied the same way. It is just an overhand knot. To make one, first hold all of your strands together. Make sure that they are not tangled. Next, bend your strands in half, all together.

In this example I am using two strands. Notice that after folding and tying your loop, you will have four strands to work with.

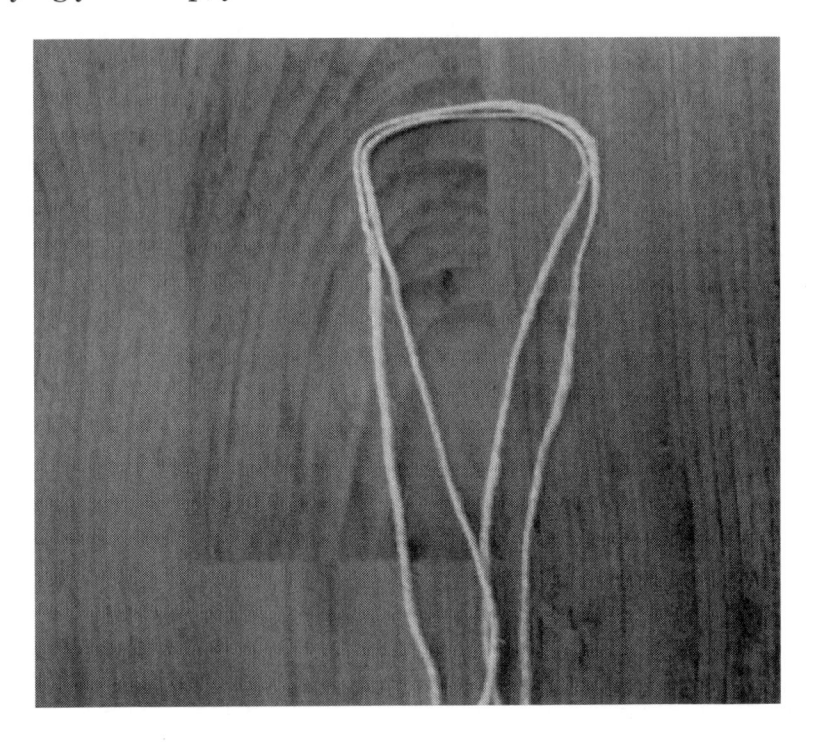

At the midpoint of your strands, make a loop and pinch it between your thumb and forefinger. The loop does not have to be very large. About the size of the tip of your ring finger should do.

I use the loop at the beginning and a bead at the end of my jewelry that the loop can hook around to fasten the jewelry when as it is worn. So it is important to consider the size of bead you are using at the end as well.

Once you have your loop secured between your thumb and forefinger, wrap the hanging strands behind and around your loop.

Bring the strands around to the new loop you created and push them through.

Next, pull tightly until the loop is the size you desire. You will not have much room to work with once the knot begins to tighten, so it is best to try and get as close to the loop size you want before tying it tight.

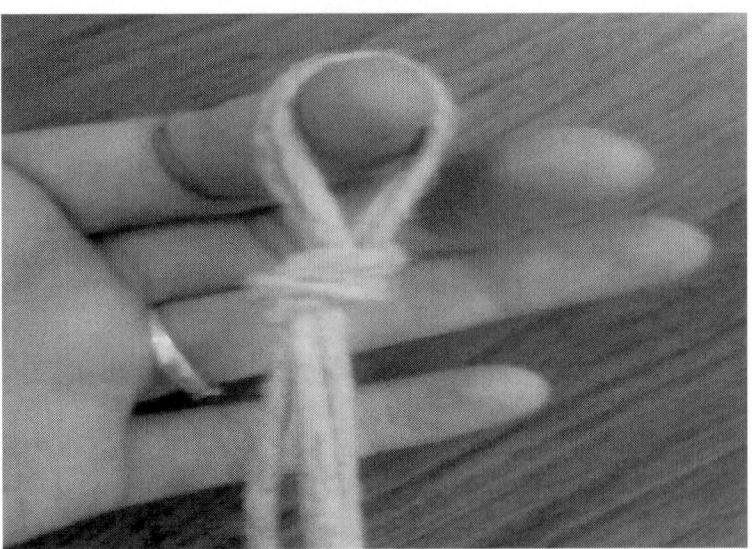

Tying the Knot

In most cases, you will be tying knots around a middle strand or strands. The rest of the strands should be split evenly at each side. If you are making a necklace, for example, you may decide you want to work with six strands. You may decide you want two strands in the middle (these will not be used to make knots), then two strands on either side. Or, you might choose to use four strings in the middle and one on either side. It just depends on how thick or thin you want your jewelry. You should experiment to find out what works best for you. Either way, you tie the outer strands around the inner strands.

When you begin making your knots, it is important that you keep your middle strands tight. This is another way your loop comes in handy. Attach your loop to something sturdy on one end, and your middle strands to something sturdy at the other end, so that you have a tight line to work with. A wooden plank with a couple of nails in it will do. In a pinch, I have been known to throw the loop around a pencil or scissors and hold it with my toe. If I have nothing to tie off to, I will hold the middle strings with my teeth. This is something I do when I am making jewelry for me or my household, as I am quite sure customers would not care too much for this less than sanitary method. Also be aware that clenching the hemp strands between your teeth is not good at all for your teeth. So, I am not condoning the method, just sharing what I do in a pinch. There are jewelry makers who would argue that keeping the middle strands tight is not necessary. However, I have found that it takes considerably more effort and time to make jewelry otherwise because of all the extra pulling and tugging that is required.

As with everything in life, there are exceptions. There are certain knots that you do not want to pull too tightly, as well as certain, more delicate designs. I will mention in the guide when it is not necessary to pull tightly.

Learning the Half Twist Knot

The half twist (sometimes called the half square) is one of the most popular knots used in hemp jewelry making. In my opinion, it is also one of the easiest, which is why I have chosen to show it first. I am right handed, so I show things from the perspective of a right handed person. If you are left handed you may be more comfortable doing the opposite. That is, if I say "start with the right strand" and you feel better starting with the left, it is perfectly ok. Just be sure to do the rest the opposite way, too.

For this example I will use four strands. Pull and cut two strands of hemp that are about a foot long each, or a length you are comfortable with. Length is not important here as you are just learning knots. Fold your strands in half and make a loop at the midpoint of the strands. You should now have four strands of equal length, or at least close in length. Again, you do not have to be exact.

Separate your strands so that you have two strands in the center and one strand on either side.

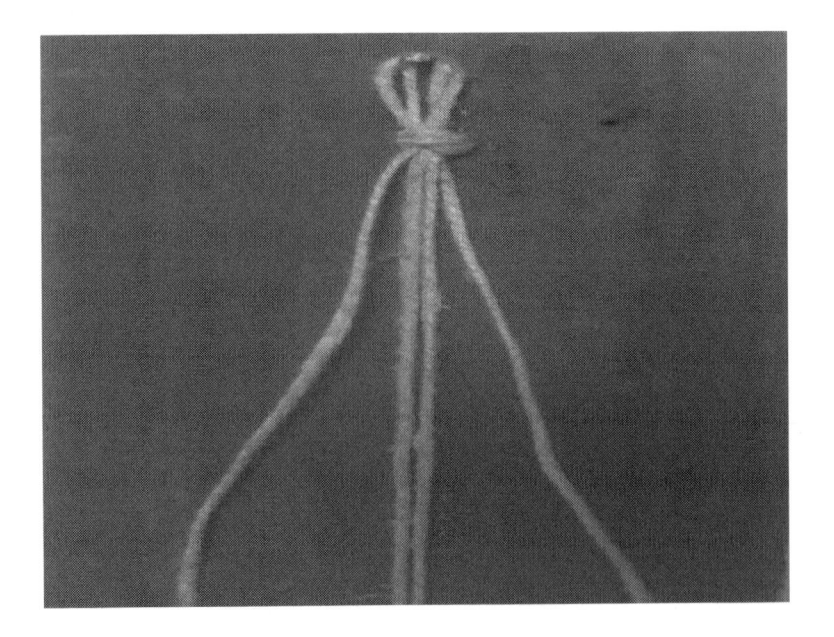

With your two middle strands tight, grab the strand on the outermost right and make a mouse ear. (I refer to it here as a mouse ear because it does not look like a rabbit ear to me.)

The strand from the right side should overlap the middle strands.

Then grab the strand on the left. Overlap the strand that is making the mouse ear. Bring the strand underneath the two middle strands, then pull it through the mouse ear on the right.

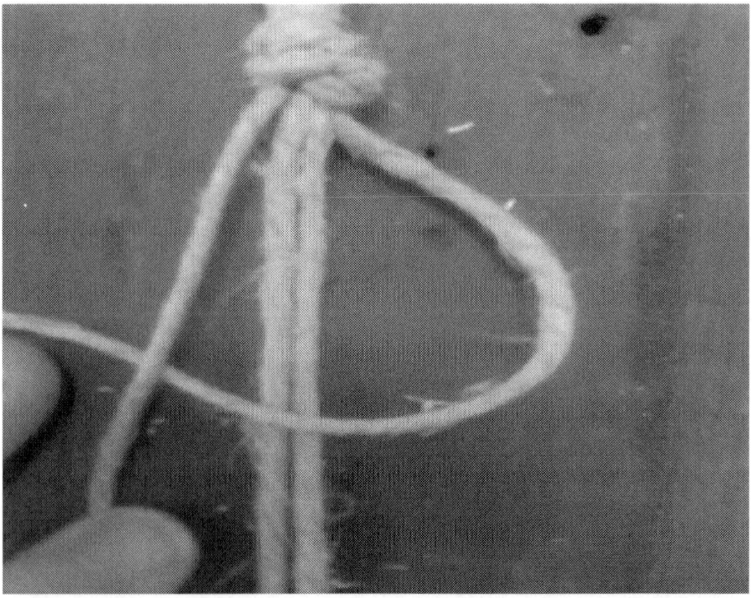

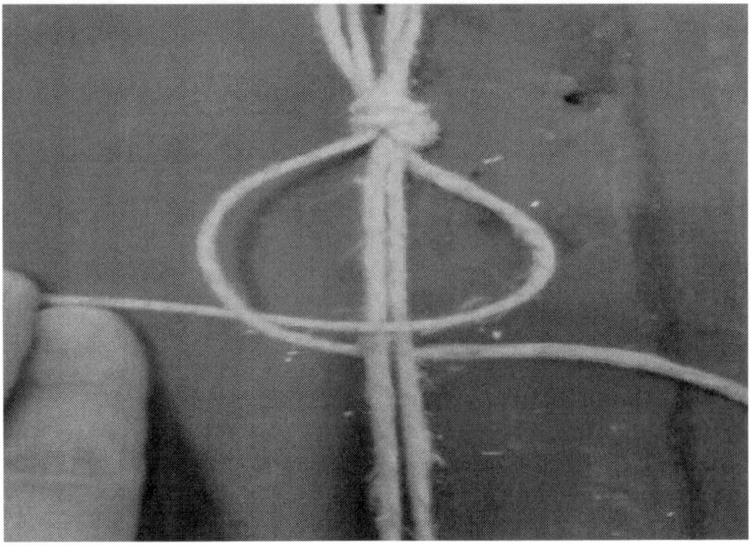

Now pull until your knot is tight.

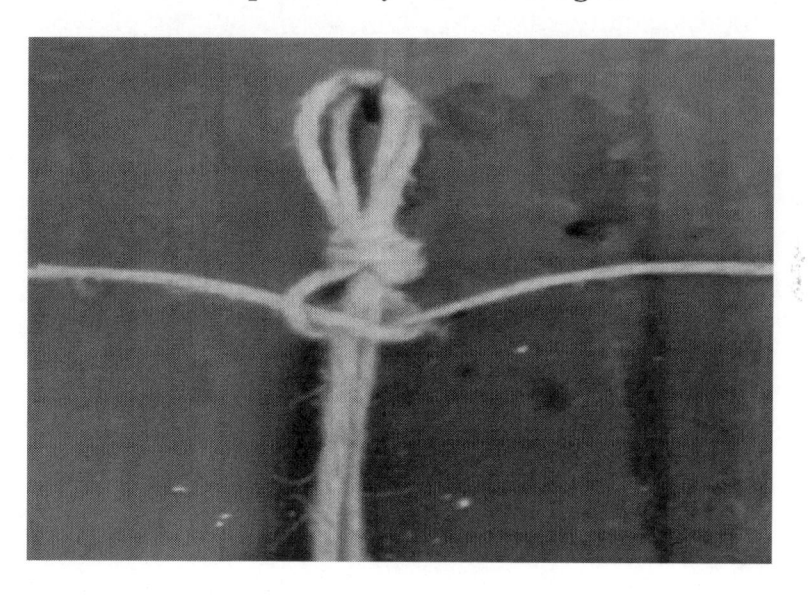

When repeated, the half twist creates a gorgeous spiral design. It looks much more complicated than it actually is.

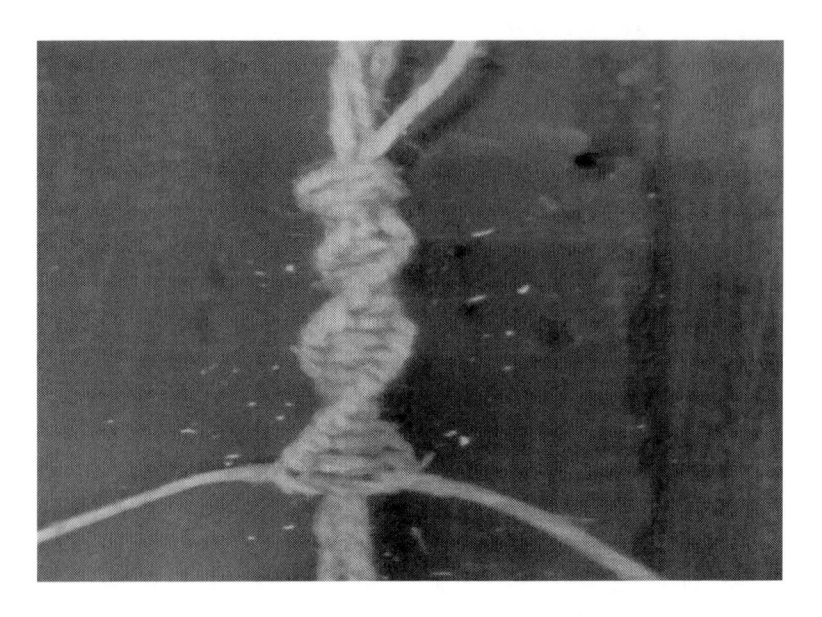

I prefer to use round or oval beads with the spiral style because it flows well. Start counting with the first half twist knot that you make. Stop the count with your first bead. When you place your first bead, restart your count and place your next bead so it is spaced the same distance as the first one according to your count. For example, if you placed your first bead after ten knots, you should place the next and subsequent beads every ten knots. This will give your jewelry a balanced look To end, tie an overhand knot. For best results, snip any long hanging strings and secure with fabric glue.

Learning the Square Knot

The square knot is essentially the same as two half twists. You simply make one half twist knot and then mirror it on the opposite side. That is to say, if you started on the right side with your first half twist, you would start on the left side with your second and vice versa. Try not to lose track of which side you last made a knot on. If you lose track it will be very noticeable in your finished piece. This is easy to do when you have a lot of distractions. If you need to stop in the middle of making your jewelry, it might be a good idea to have sticky notes handy so that you can write down your knot count and what side you were on when you left off.

Here is an example using four strands.

Begin as you did with the half twist knot.

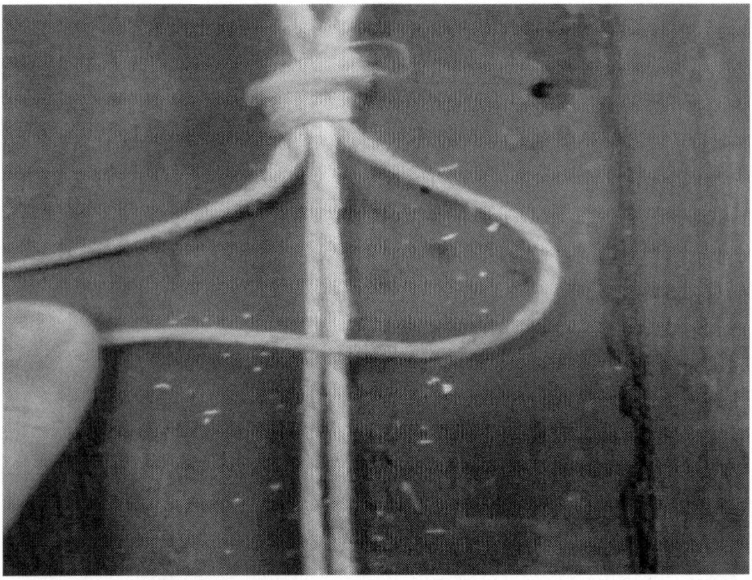

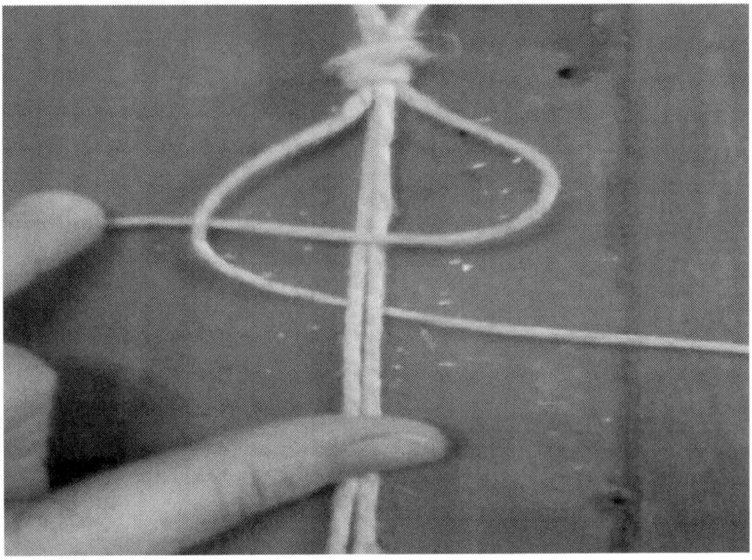

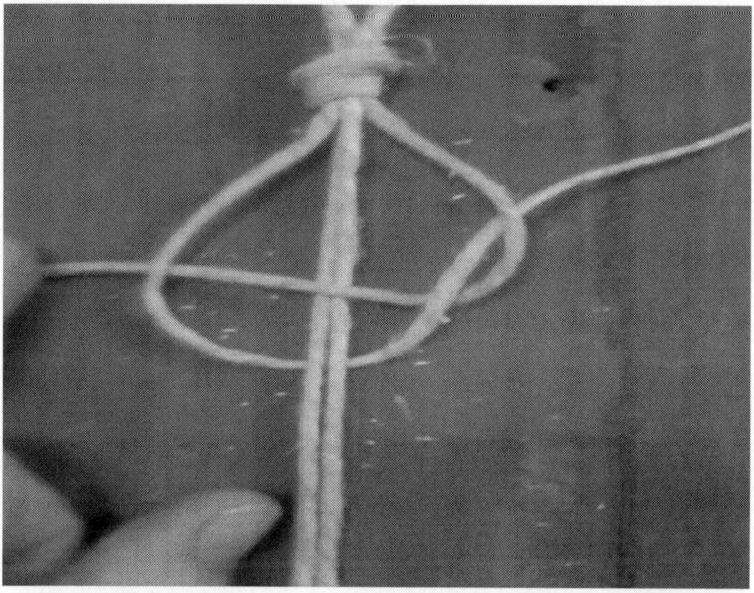

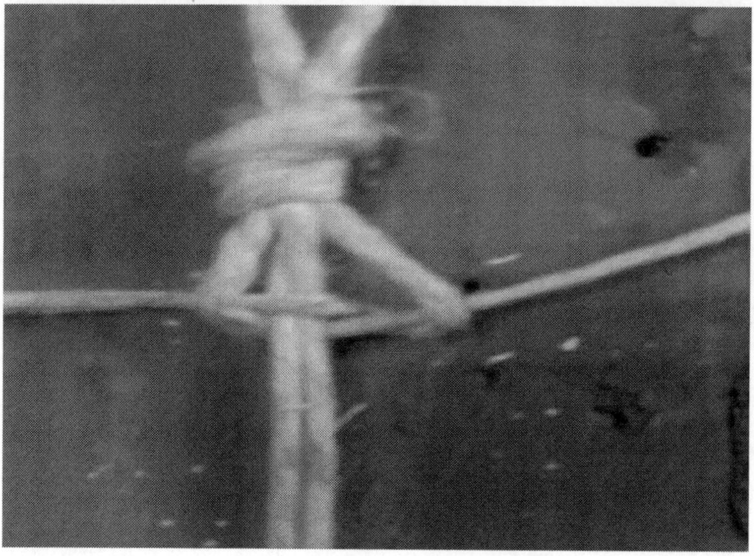

Now, mirror the fist half knot. Start on the opposite side.

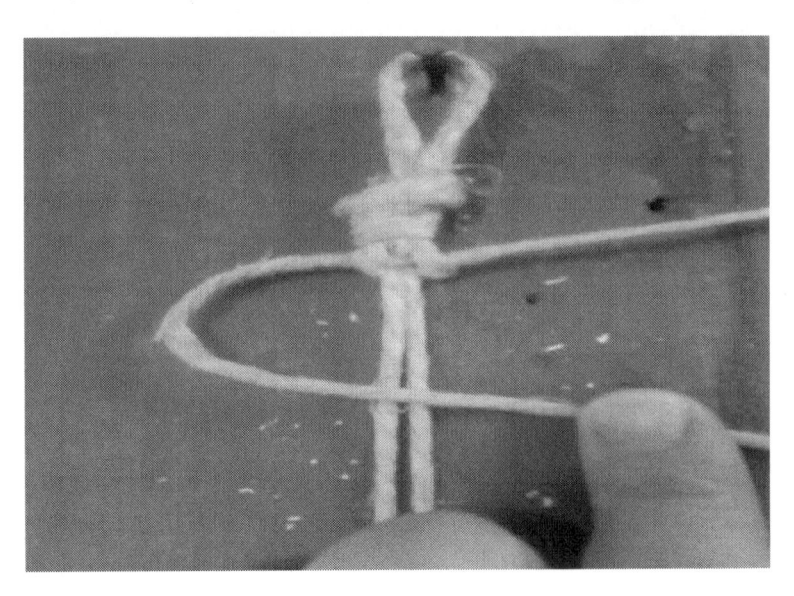

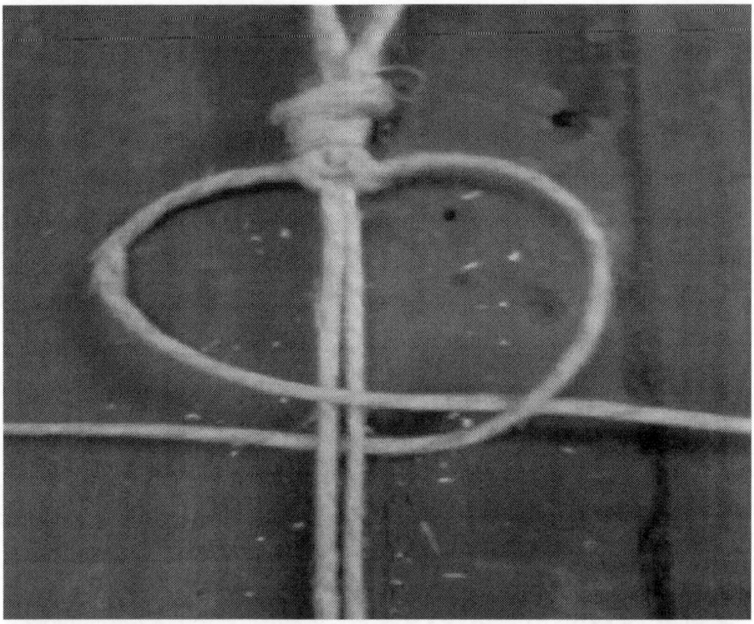

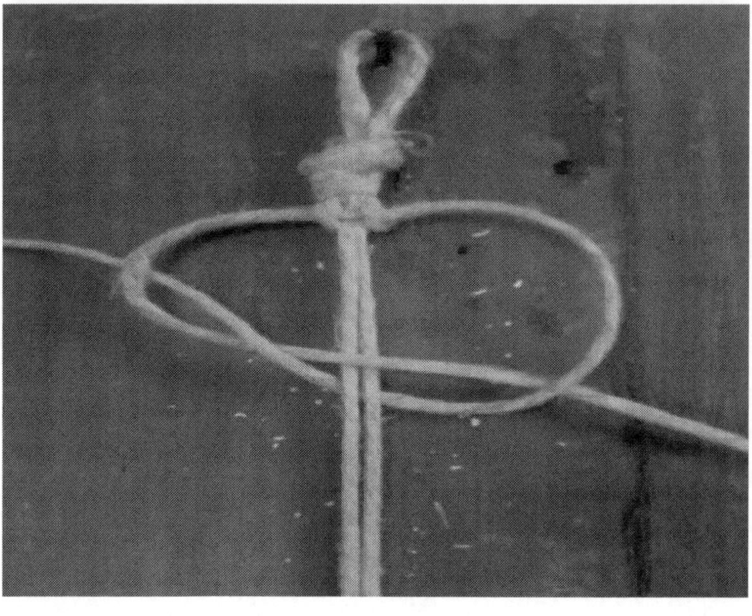

Pulling tight, you should have two half twist knots that mirror each other, or one square knot.

Repeating the square knot gives a flat, weaved look. It is very versatile and easy to combine with other knots to create a very unique appearance.

41

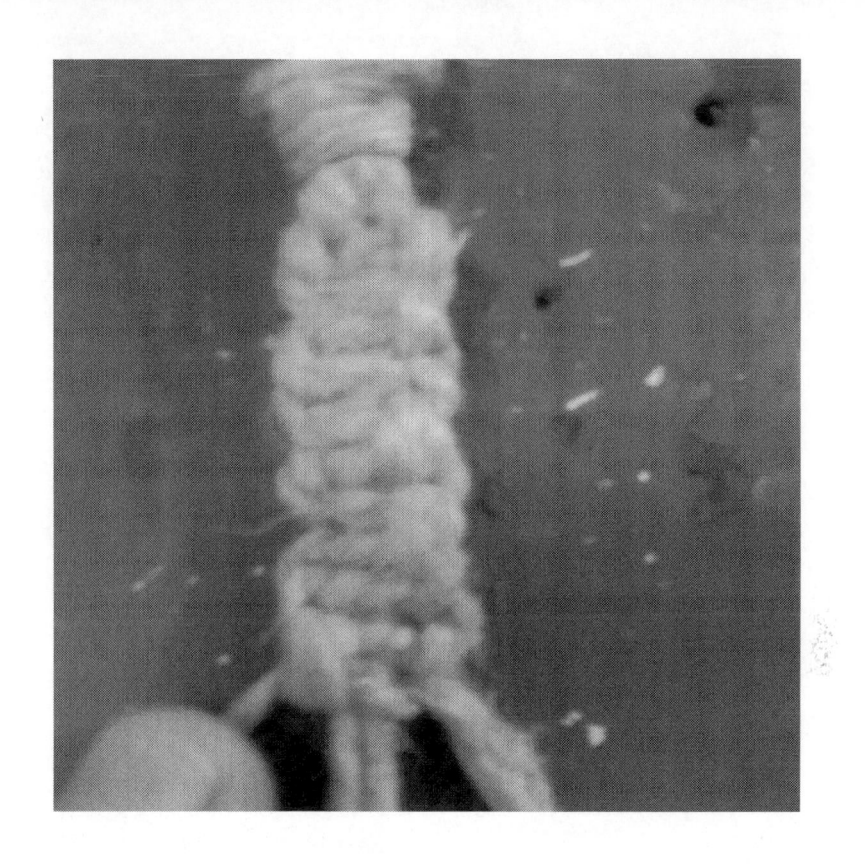

Learning the Half Hitch Knot

This is an extremely simple knot. I will use three strands of hemp in this example. To get three strands as shown in the picture below, pull one strand that is of your desired length, and pull another strand that is twice the length of your first strand. Again, length does not matter here as this is practice. Tie an overhand knot in the beginning of your shorter strand. Fold the second strand in half to make a loop and place the knotted end of your first strand in the center of the loop. Now make an overhand knot just as you have in the other examples.

Here, you will notice that unlike other knots, you are not using just the middle strand to make knots around.

First, grasp the two strings on the right.

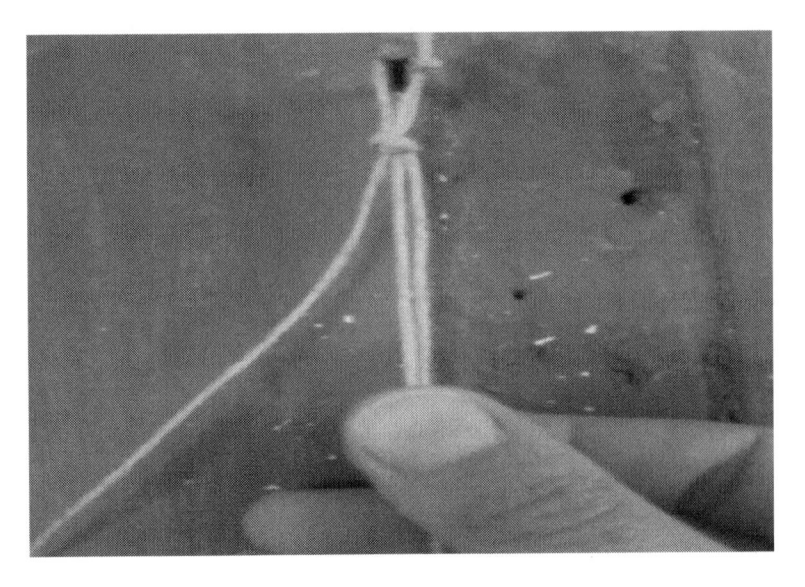

Take the remaining string and go over and around the first two, then through the mouseear that you created.

That's it! Pull tight and repeat the pattern.

44

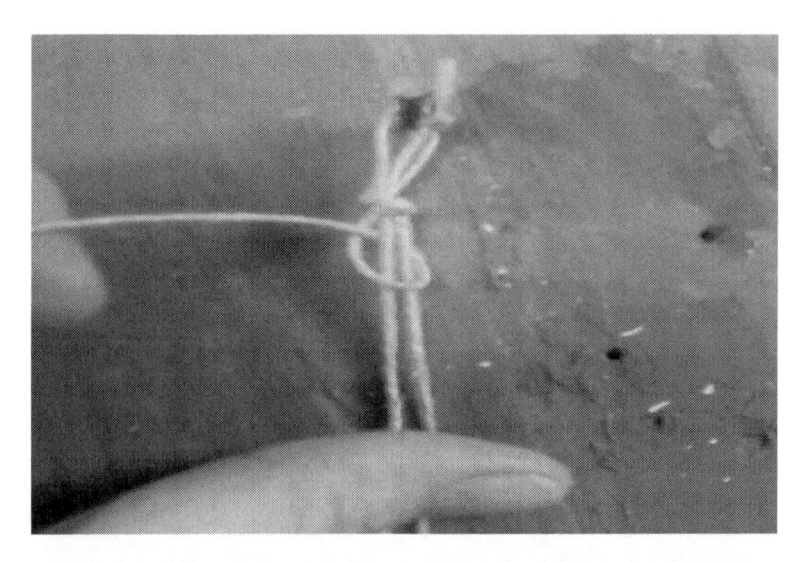

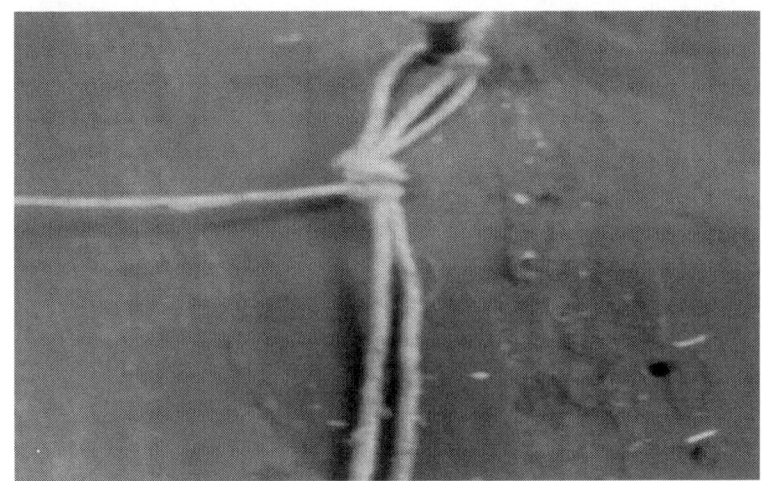

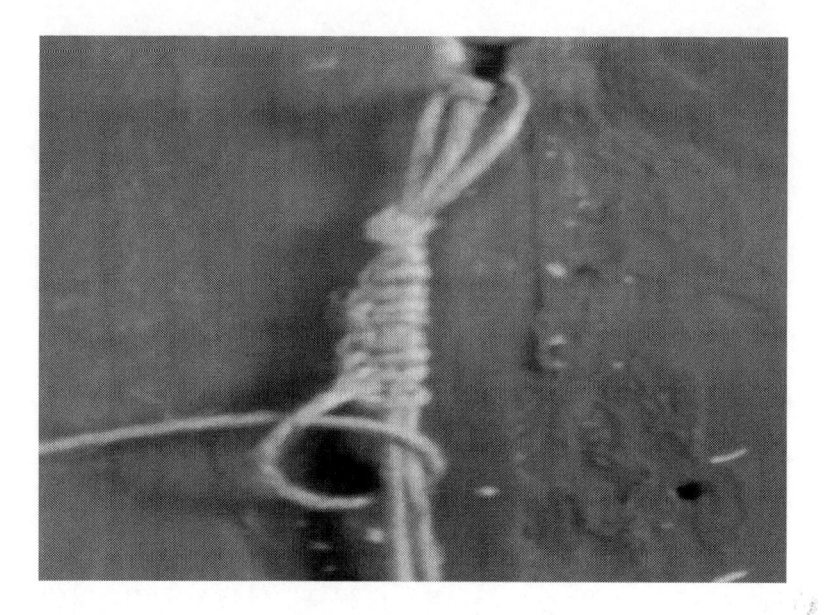

Important side note: You do not want to pull your half hitch knots too tightly, as they will bunch up. Just pull enough to bring your knots close together. Push up from the bottom frequently.

Learning the Alternating Half Hitch Knot

I will also use three stands in this example. Pull one strand to your desired length, then pull another strand twice that length. Fold your longer strand in half, place your shorter strand in the center of your loop, and tie an overhand knot as you did in the last example.

Note: You do not absolutely have to tie a knot in the beginning of your shorter strand, as the overhand knot in the loop should hold your strand in place. Personally, I have never used the extra knot in the shorter strand, and I've never had a problem. However, a lot of people prefer to do this as an extra measure to ensure that the strand will not slip. That is why I included it in the last example.

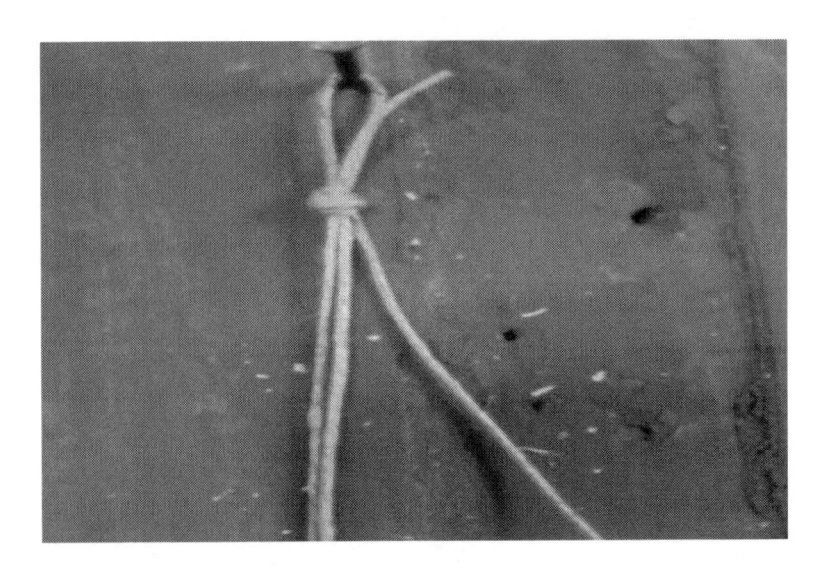

Separate your strands so that you have two strands on the left and one strand on theright, as shown in the picture above.

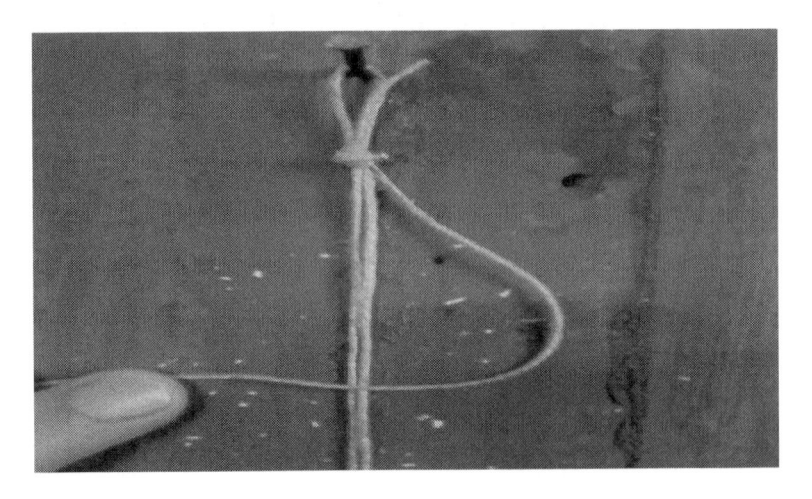

Using the strand on the right, make a mouse ear. Your right strand should lay over the top of the other two strands.

Pull your strand underneath the other two strands and through the mouse ear that you created.

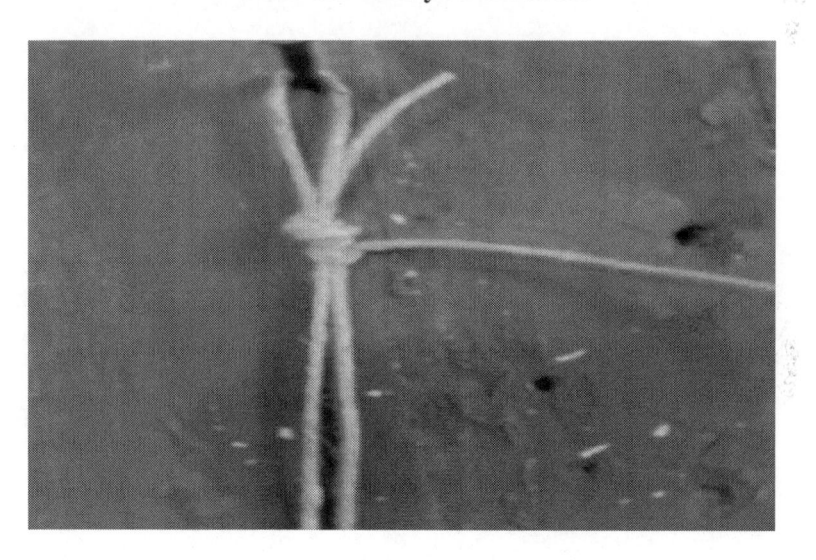

Now pull and tighten your knot.

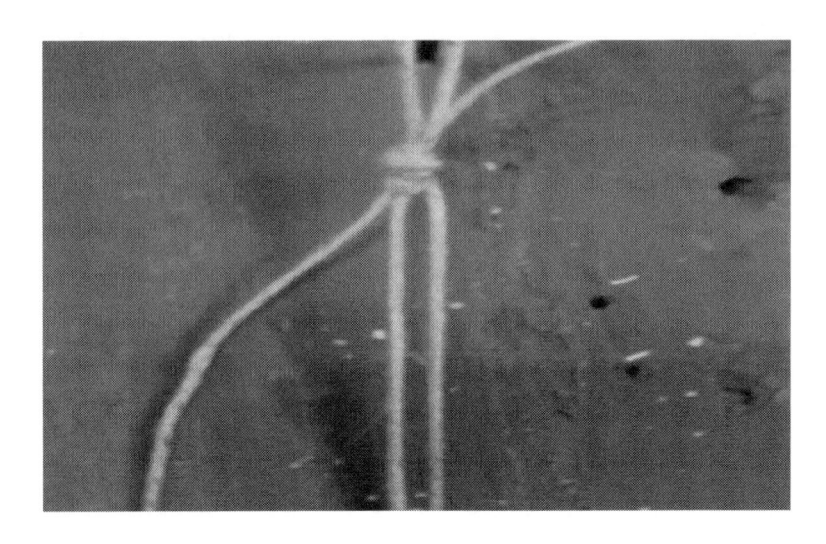

Separate your strands again. This time place two strands on the right and one on the left, as shown above.

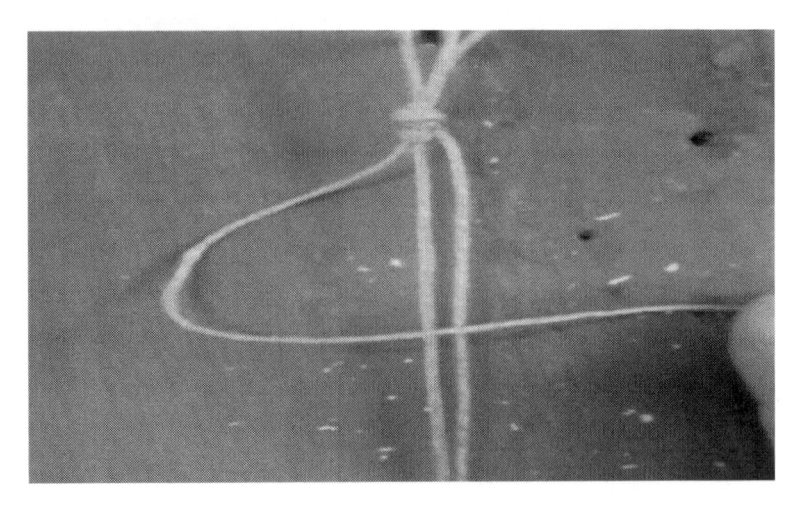

Make a mouse ear using the left strand. Your strand should again lay atop the other two strands.

Pull your strand underneath the other two strands and through the mouse ear and pull tight, as you did with the last knot.

Repeat the pattern alternating from right to left. You should end up with a chain look, as shown above.

Learning the Overhand Knot

The overhand knot is extremely common in the art of macramé. This knot is very similar to the half hitch. Except that instead of wrapping one string around another, you loop the string over and through itself. This is the same knot that you use to begin most of the jewelry presented in this guide. In this example, I am using only one strand.

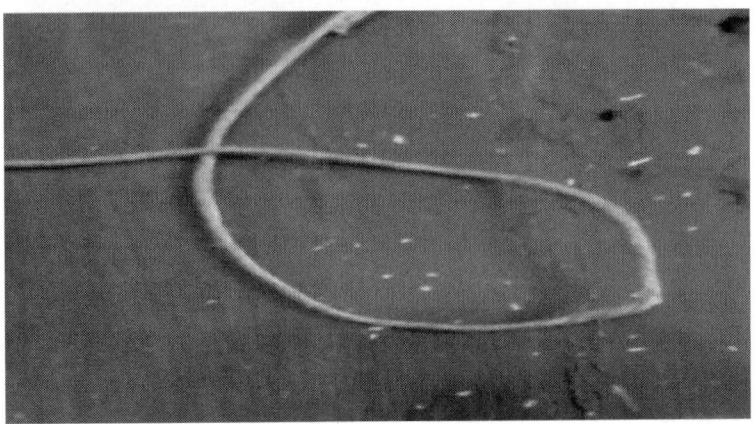

Lay the strand over itself, creating a mouse ear.

Bring your strand around and through the mouse ear.

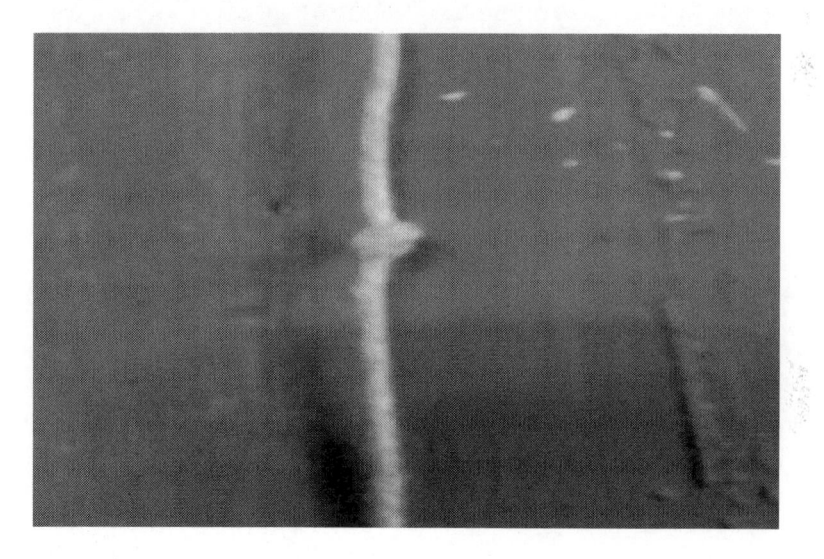

Pull your knot tight.

Repeat the knot. You can space the knots as far apart as you want, just try and keep even spacing.

Using What You Have Learned

Applying the knots you have learned thus far, you can make some fantastic jewelry pieces. A little imagination can go a long way. Do not be afraid to experiment with different styles, knots, and beads. In the next chapter I will go over different styles of bracelets and necklaces that use the knots in this chapter to give you a better idea of the results you will get.

Chapter Review

- When deciding the length of your strands, remember that it is always better to have more length than you think you will need. You can always trim excess, but you cannot add.
- You will need more length when working with thick hemp than thinner hemp.
- Keeping your middle strands tight will make it easier to tie knots with your knotting strands.

- You can make fantastic jewelry using only basic knots.
- Do not be afraid to experiment or use different knots in the same piece. The possibilities are endless!

Chapter 3: The Half Twist

Alternating Half Twist Anklet

For this anklet I will use eight strands. Pull and cut four strands of hemp that are about six times your desired anklet length, plus an additional foot or so. Fold the strands in half to make a loop, and tie an overhand knot.

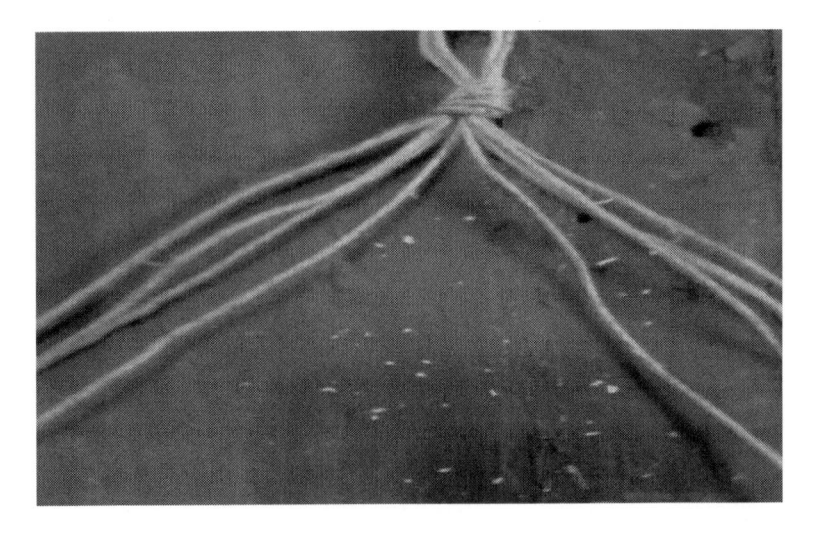

Begin by separating your strands so that you have four strands on the left and four strands on the right.

Start with the four strands on the left. Use the two outer strands to make six half twist knots around the two middle ones.

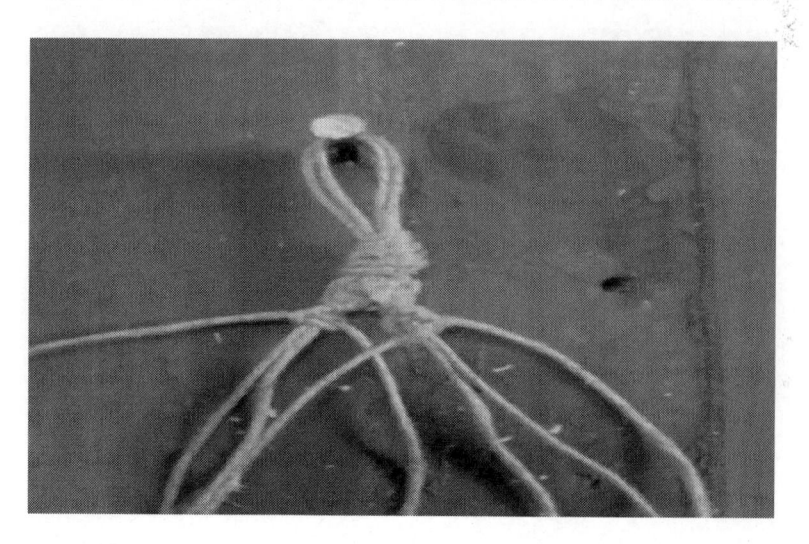

Do the same using the four remaining strands on the right side.

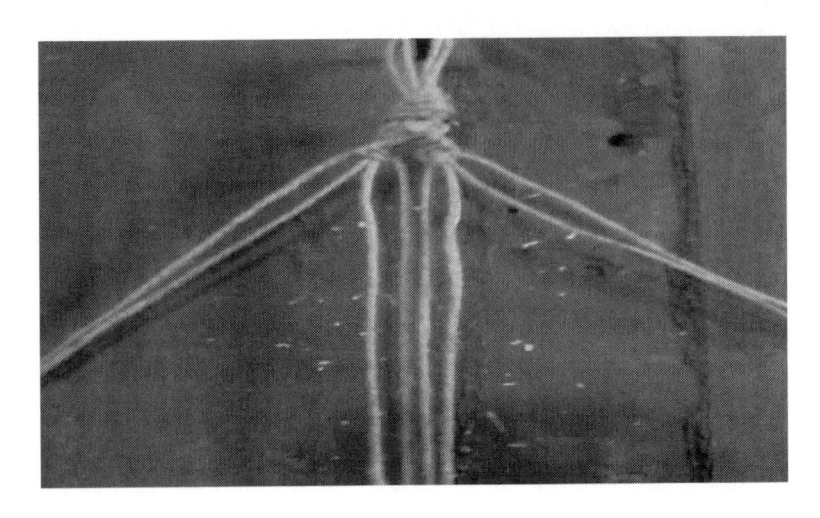

Separate your strands so that you have four in the middle and two on either side of the four.

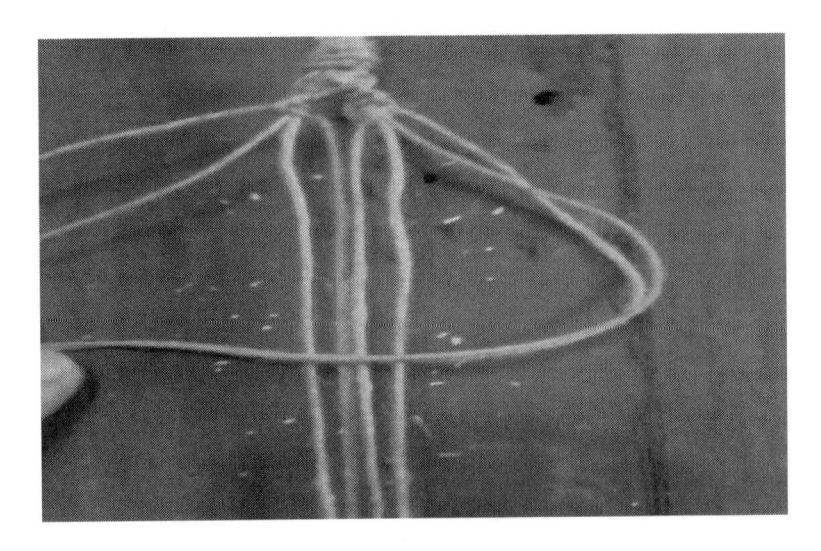

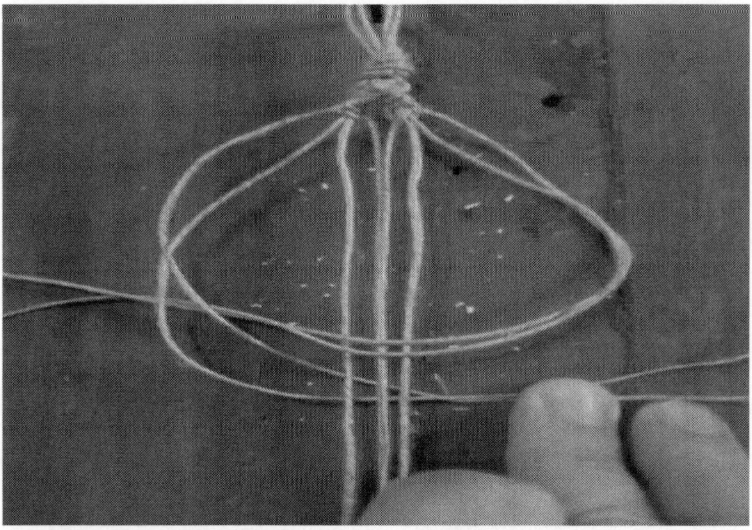

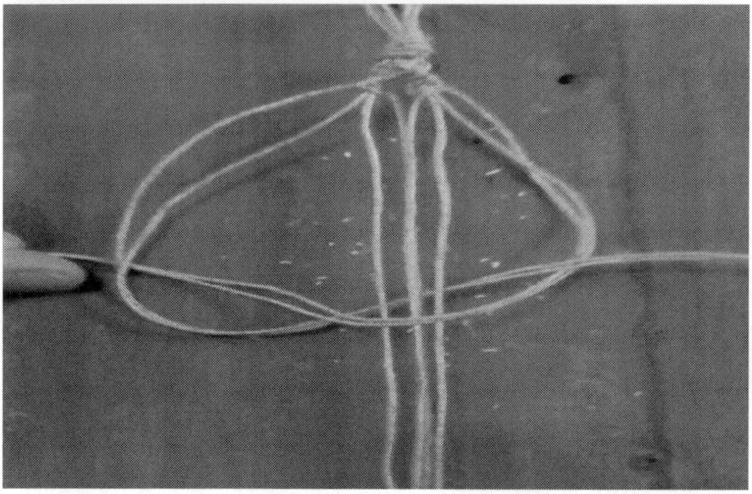

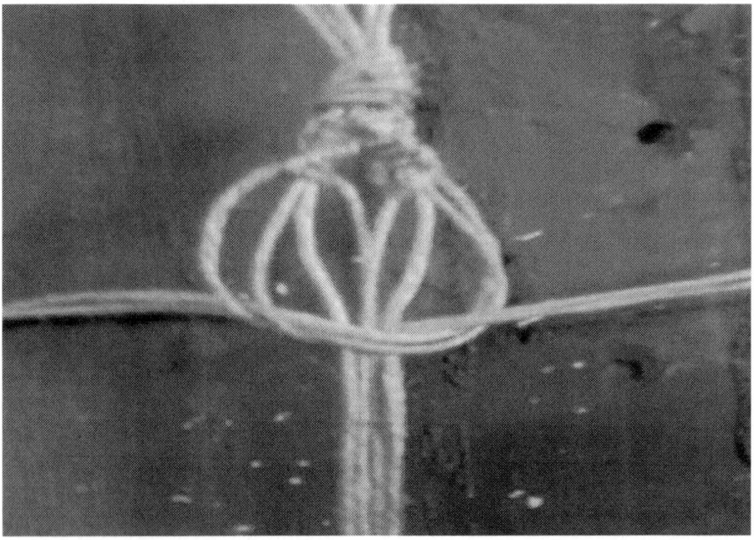

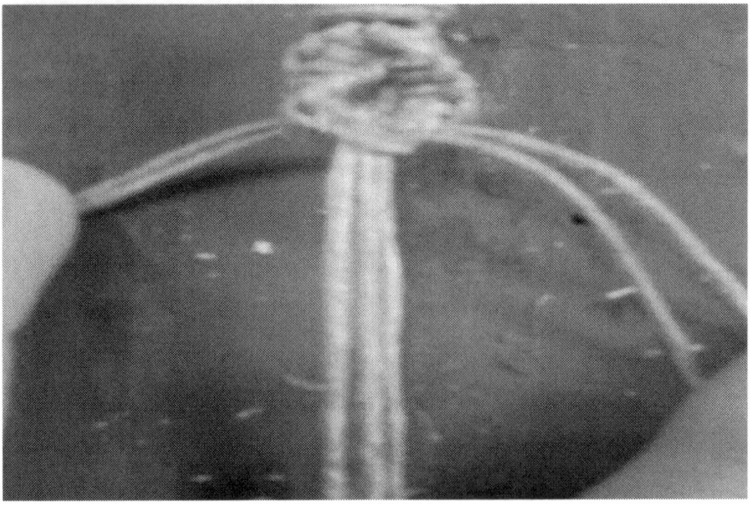

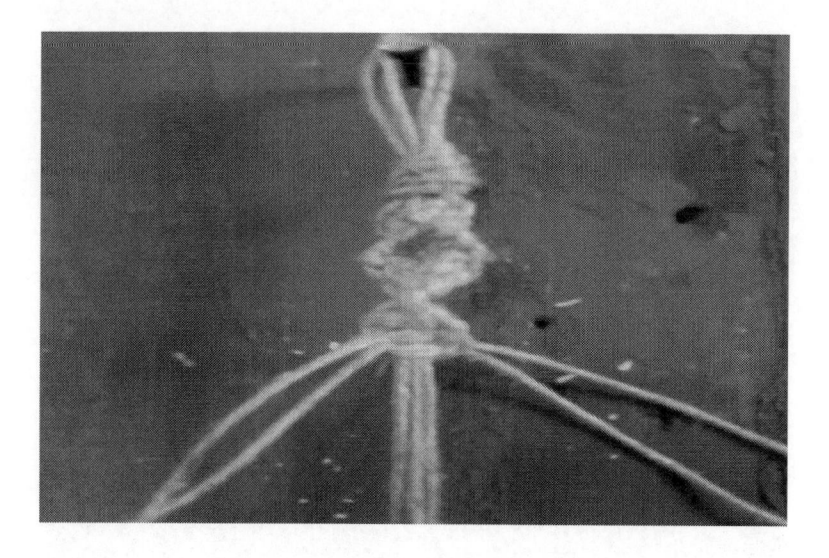

Tie six half twist knots using the two strands on either side, as shown above.

Separate the strands again so that you have four strands on the left and four strands on the right. Again, make six half twist knots with the four strands on the left and six half twist knots with the strands on the right.

Continue this pattern for the entire anklet.

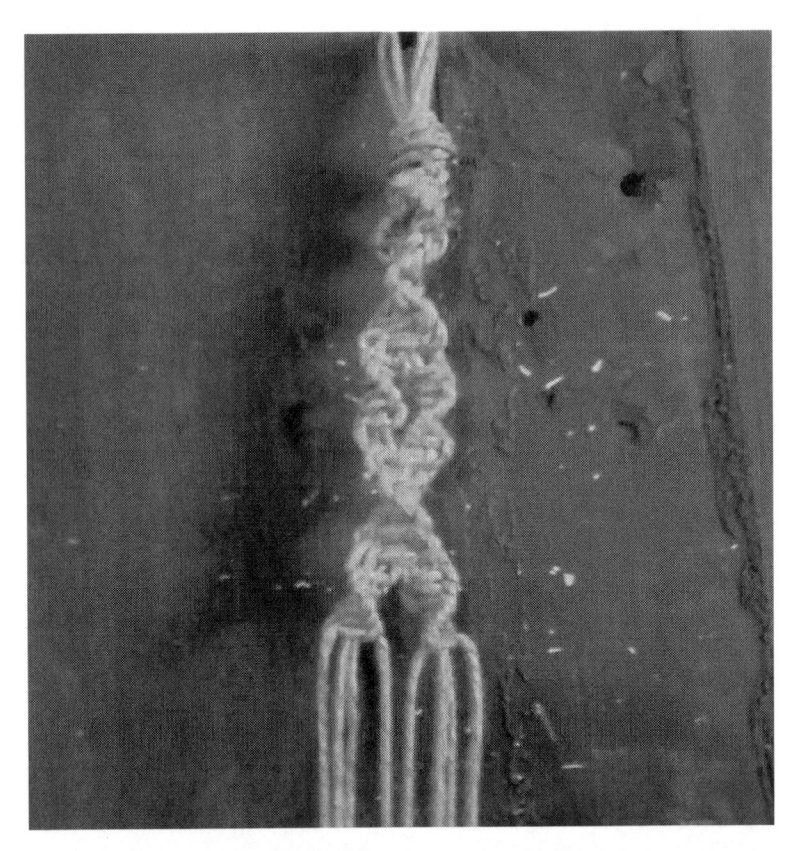

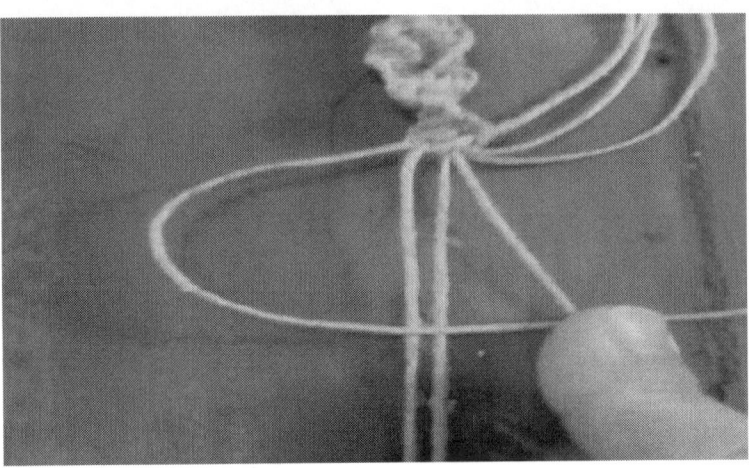

Tip: If you start with your mouse ear on the left on one side, start with your mouse ears on the right for the other side. This is optional and just creates symmetry. It only applies when you are working with four strands on either side. If that sounds complicated, just do all of your knots in the same direction. You will still have a great anklet in the end.

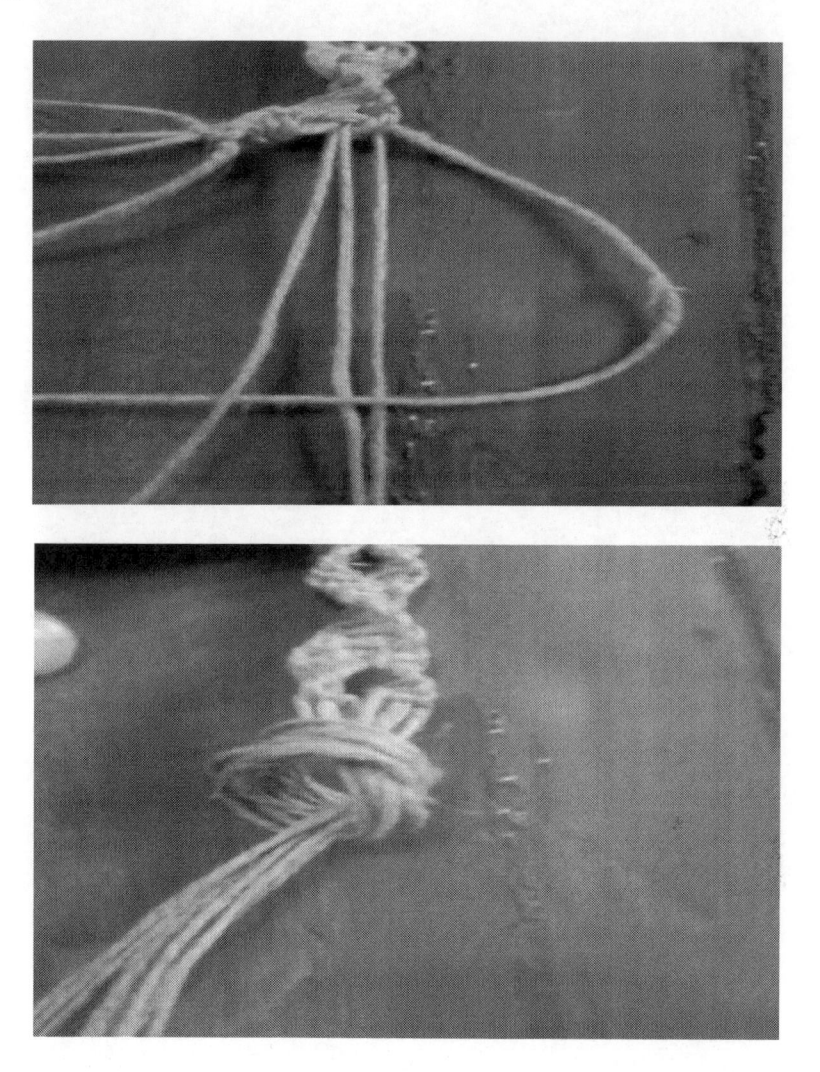

End your anklet by making an overhand knot.

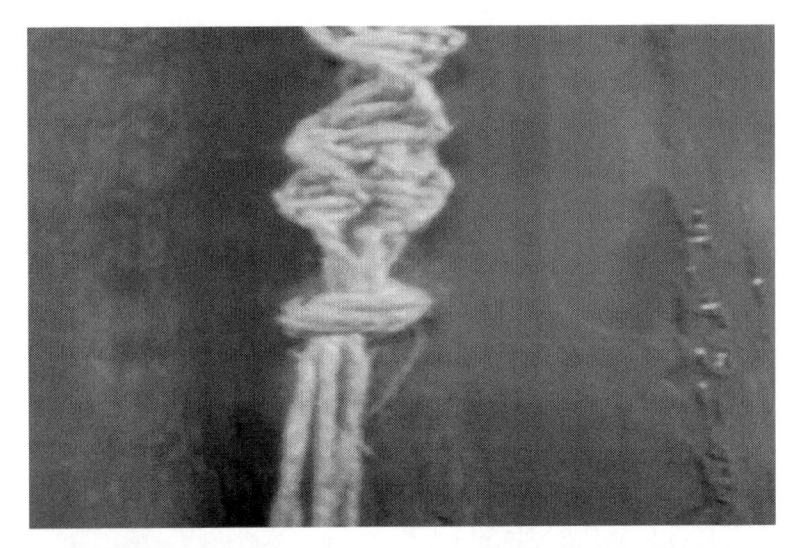

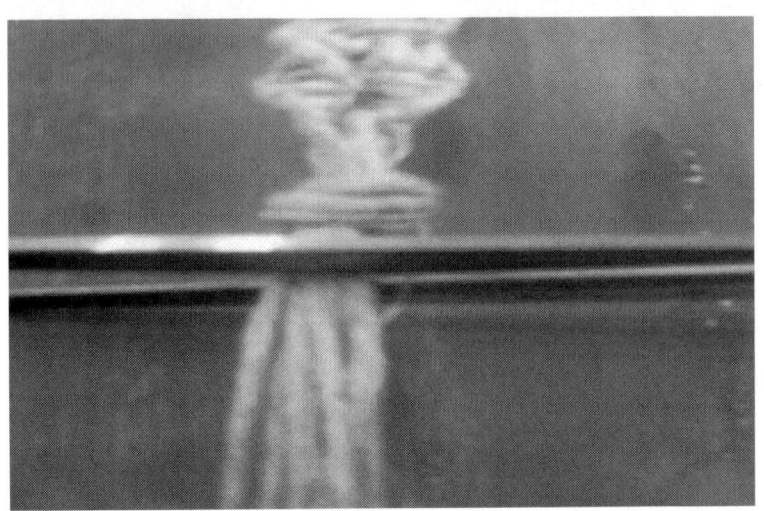

Cut away excess material.

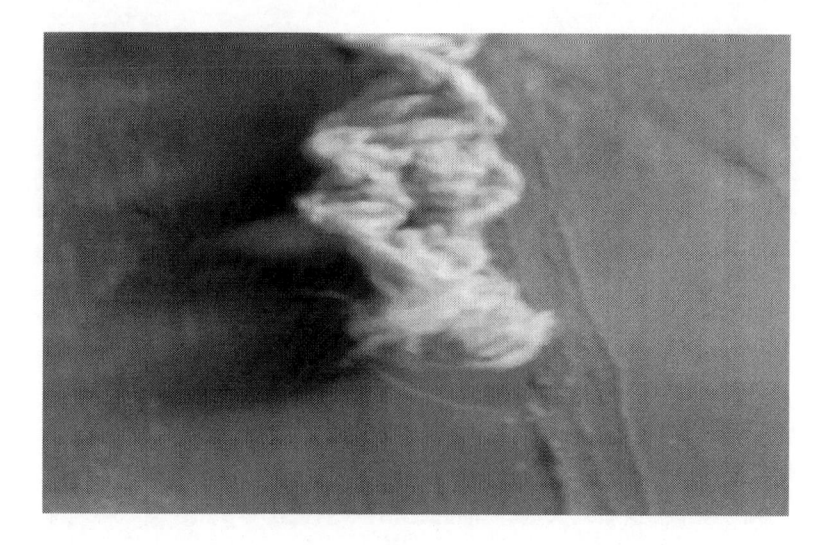

Secure your knot with fabric glue and allow to dry.

Use the loop and knot to close your anklet.

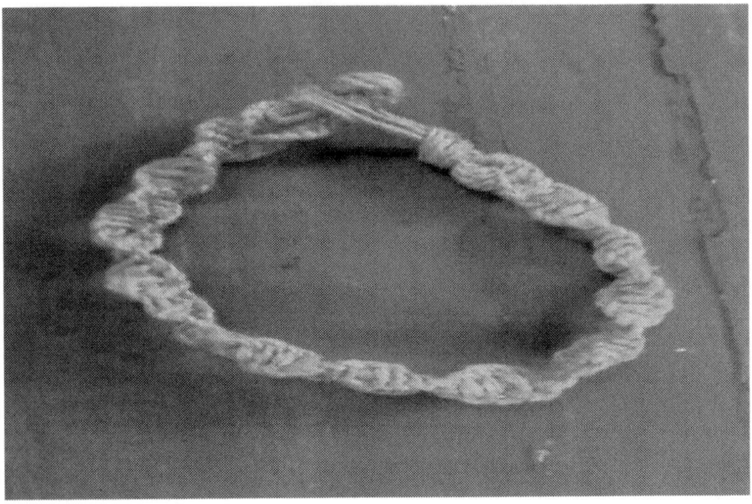

Simple Half Twist Bracelet With Beads

As the name suggests, this is a very simple bracelet. I will use four strands for this bracelet. Pull two strands of hemp about six times your desired length, plus another foot. Begin, of course by folding your strands in half, making a loop and securing it with an overhand knot. Use the two outer strands to make ten half twist knots.

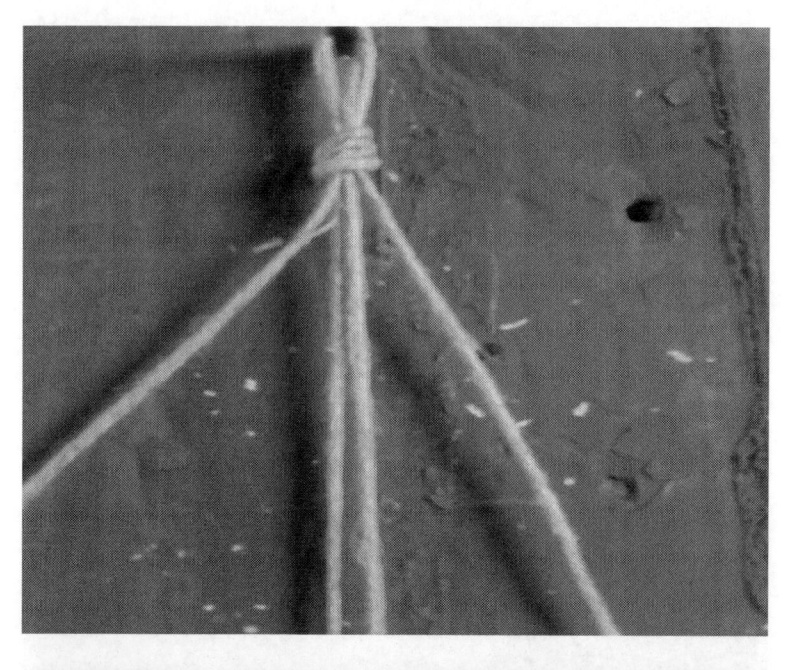

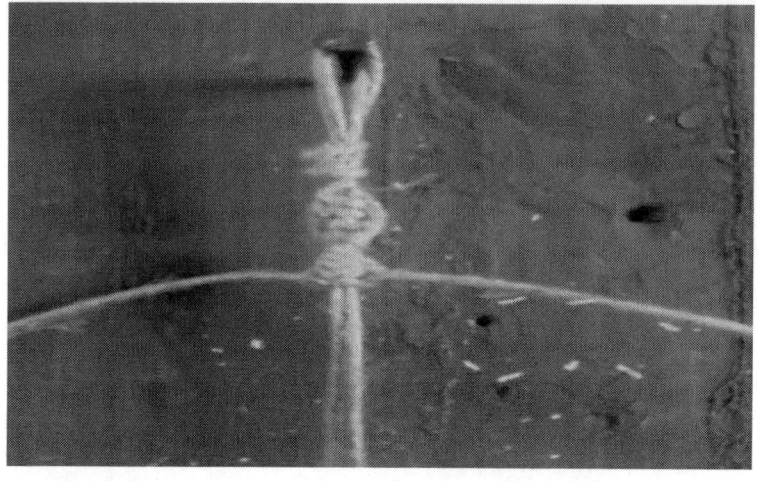

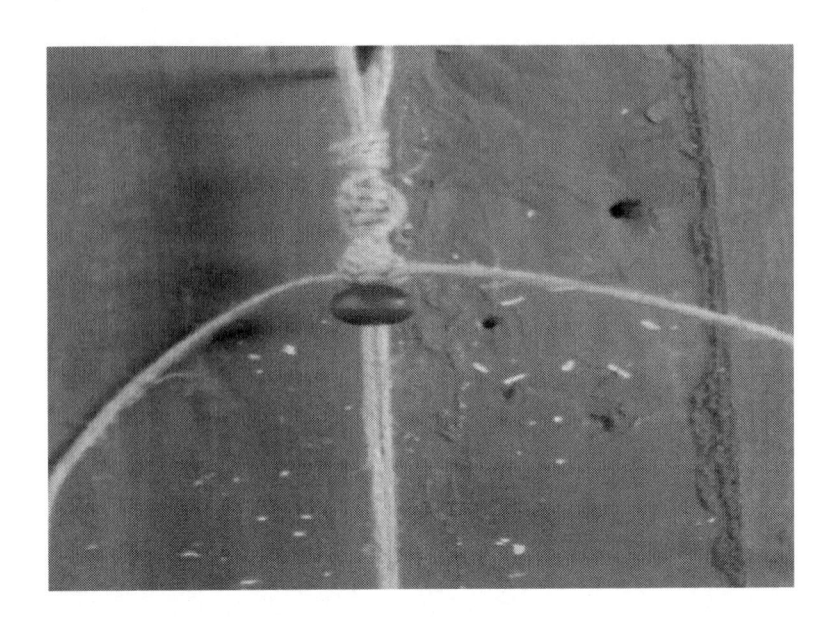

Then string a bead onto the two middle strands. Restart your count to make another ten half twist knots, and string another bead.

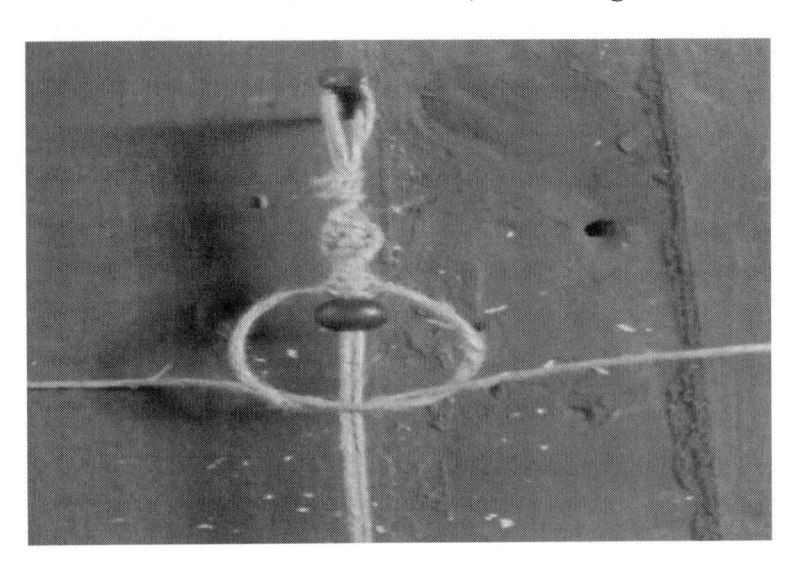

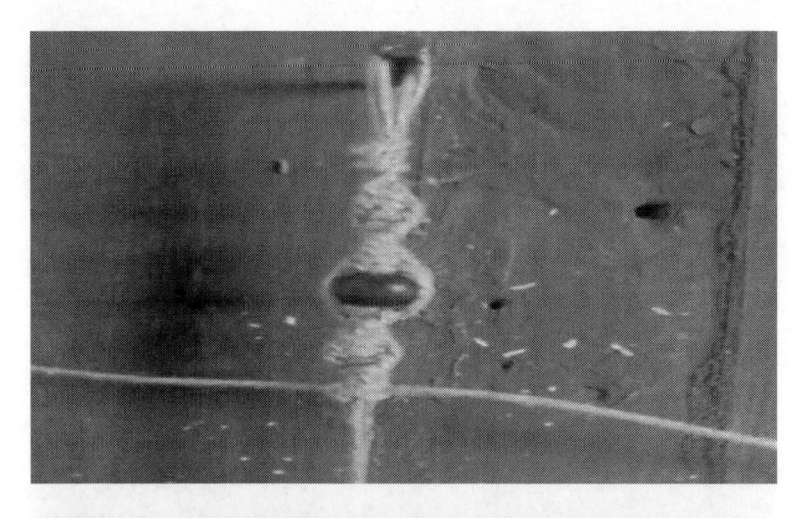

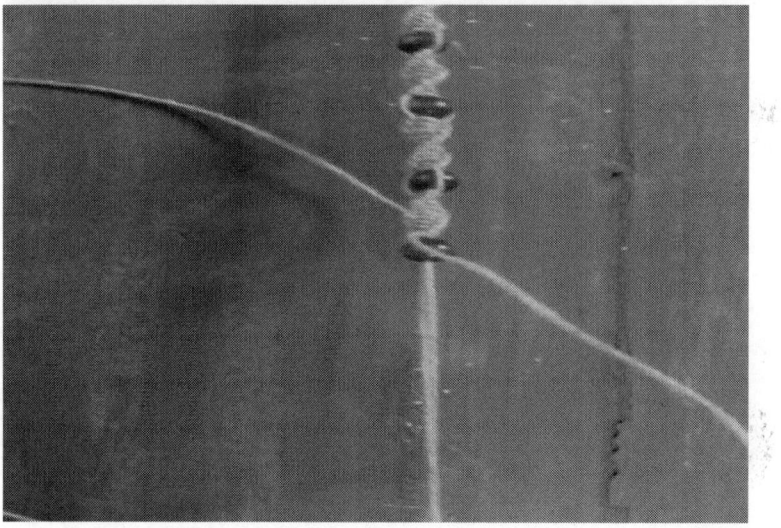

As you work, your knotting strings will twist around your middle strands. Just allow the strings to do so instead of trying to fight with them. You will lose the battle.

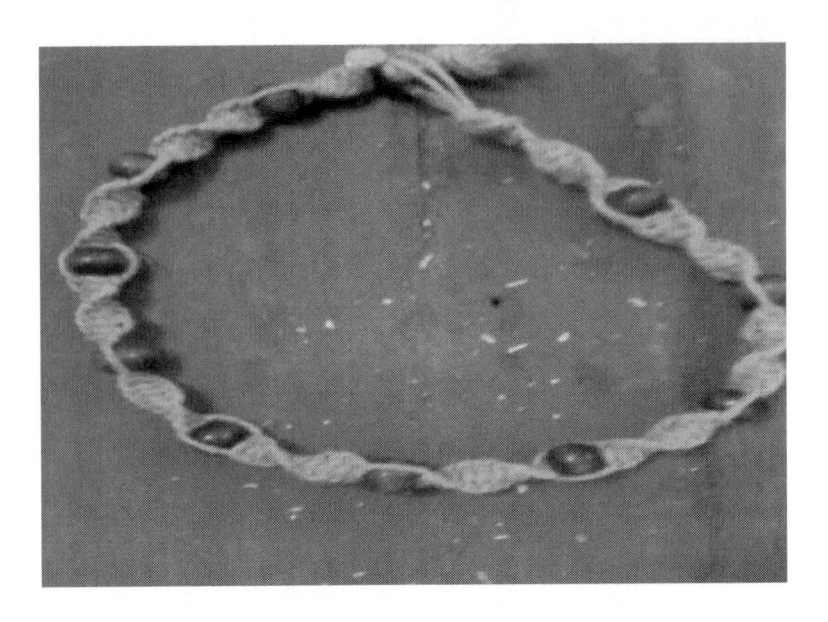

Repeat this pattern until you have achieved your desired length. End by making an overhand knot. Cut away excess string and secure the knot with fabric glue.

Examples of The Square Knot

The Fishbone

This design is aptly named. As you work, notice that your strands actually resemble the bones of a fish. The finished product also resembles the fish bones that you see in cartoons, such as when the alley cat pulls one out of the trash. The fishbone is actually one of my favorite designs to make.

Because this pattern is so delicate, I prefer to use waxed hemp with it, though I have not always done so. Waxed hemp stands up a little better to moisture than natural hemp does. The waxed hemp also feels less irritating on your skin. This design will not stand up against getting totally wet, whether you use waxed hemp or not, so be sure to remove this piece before swimming or bathing.

For this one, you will need eight strands. Pull and cut four strands of hemp that are about six times your desired length, plus another foot. Fold all of your strands in half, make a loop, and secure with an overhand knot.

To start, pull the two center strands tight. I am using dyed hemp here so that you can easily see which strands to use.

Taking the first pink inner strand on either side (next to the center strands), tie a square knot.

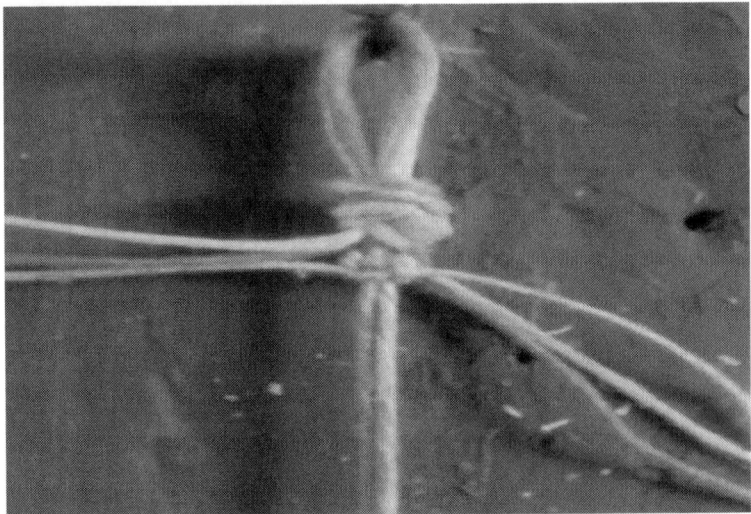

Do the same with the orange second set and yellow third, working your way from the inside out.

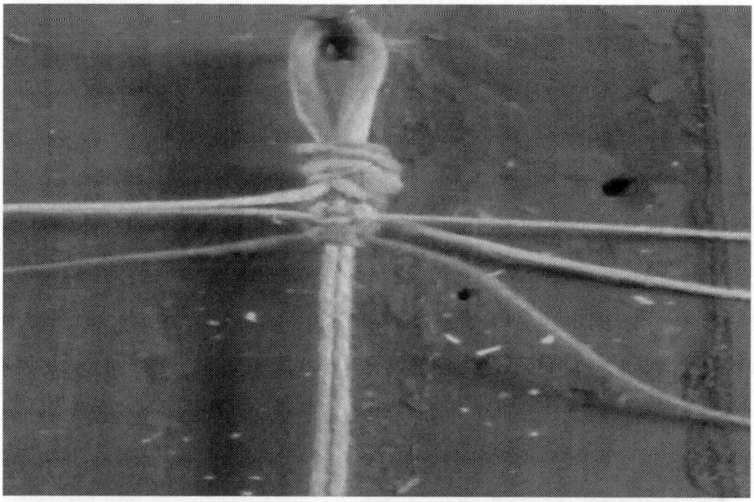

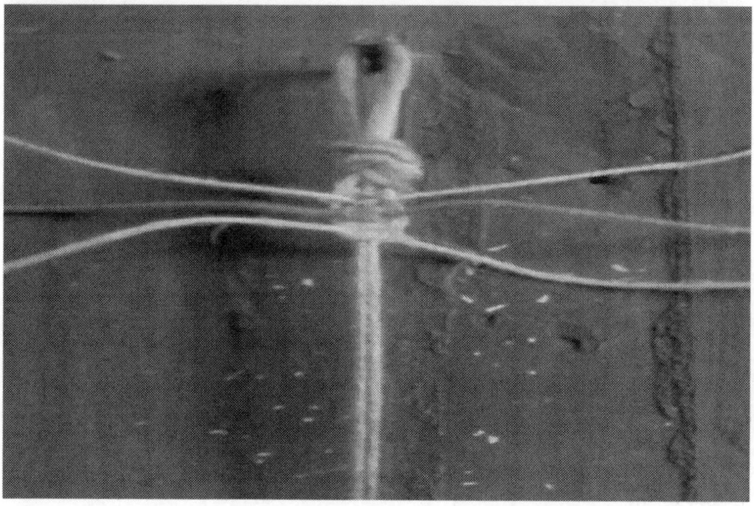

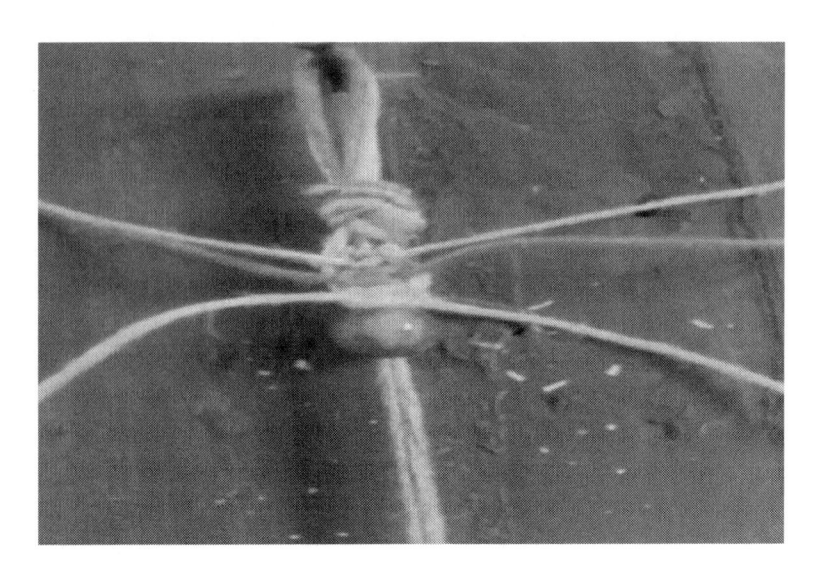

Now, using the center strands, string your first bead.

Starting with the bottom two yellow strands, tie a square knot, leaving enough slack so that you have a circle.

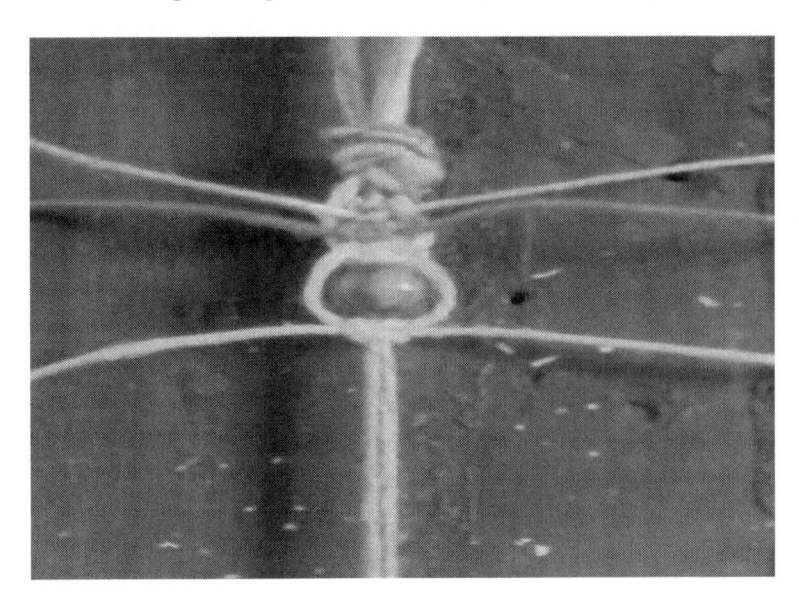

Repeat this process twice more, always starting with the bottom strands (the pink ones in this picture). When you have tied three square knots, string another bead and start again with the bottom strands.

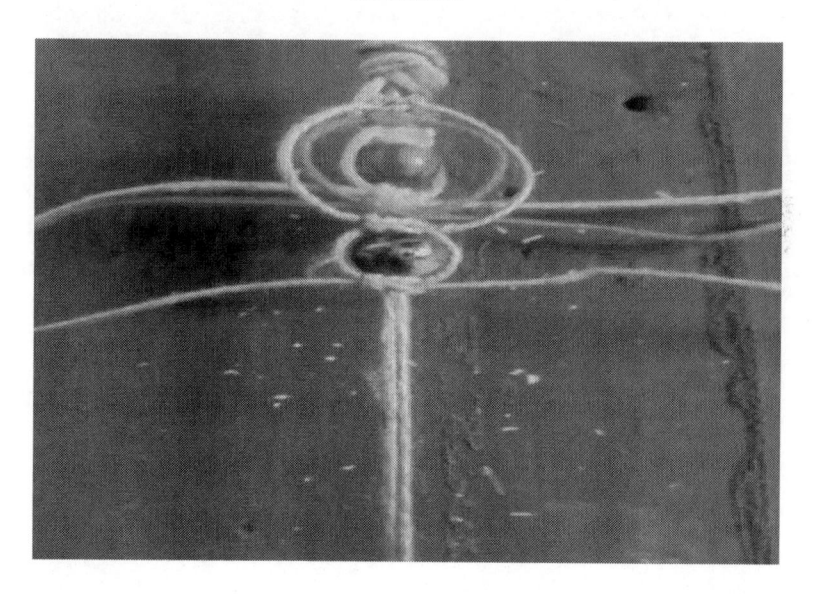

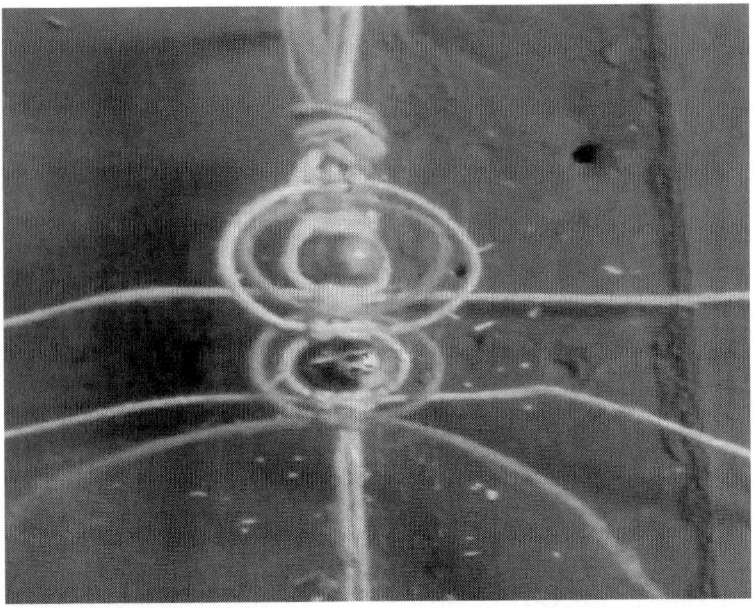

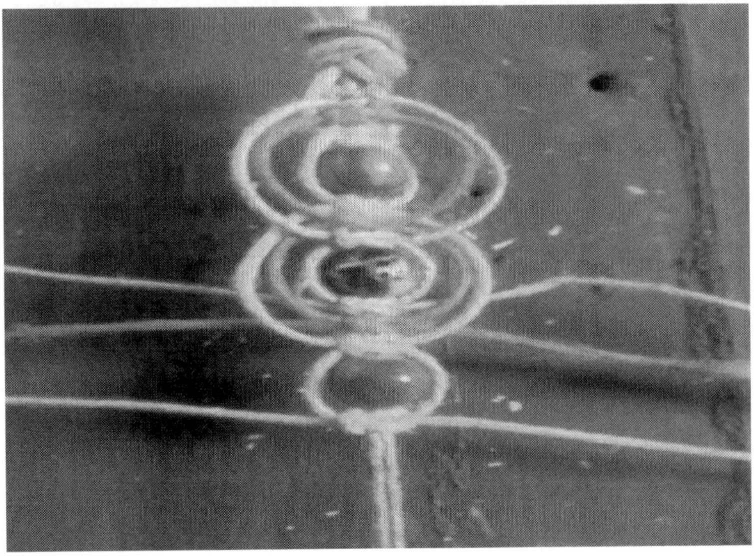

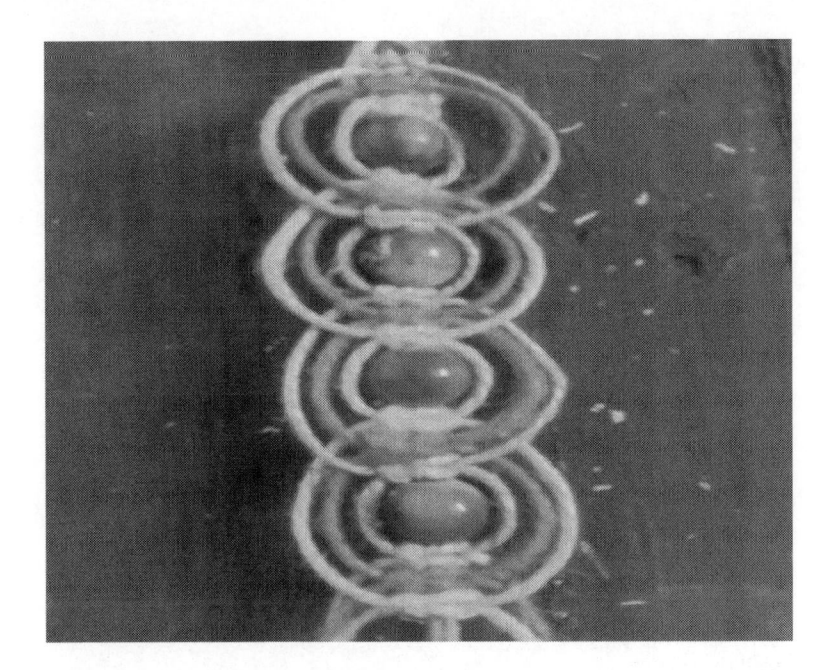

When repeated, you have the pattern shown above. Notice that the strands rotate to make an alternating pattern when you use colors.

To finish, tie three square knots as you did to begin the piece, then tie an overhand knot at the very end. Snip away any excess strand and secure your knot with fabric glue.

Choker With Square Knot Variation

For this example I will use four strands. Pull two hemp strands about six times your desired length. Fold the strands in half and tie a loop with an overhand knot. Separate your strands so that you have two strands in the middle and one on either side.

Begin by making three square knots, using the two outer strands to make the knots around the two inner strands.

Reverse your strands so that your two inner strands are now the outer strands, and the outer strands are now the middle strands. This is sometimes referred to as making an inside-out square knot.

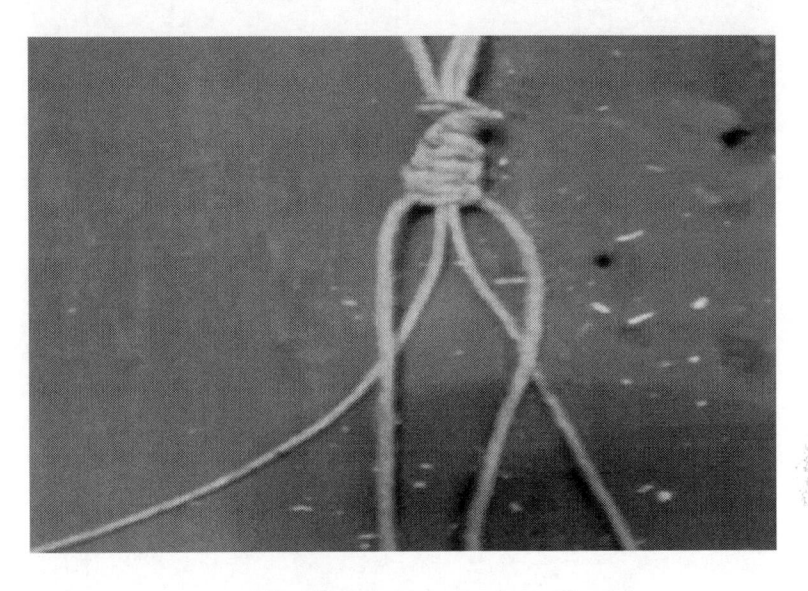

Now make three more square knots.

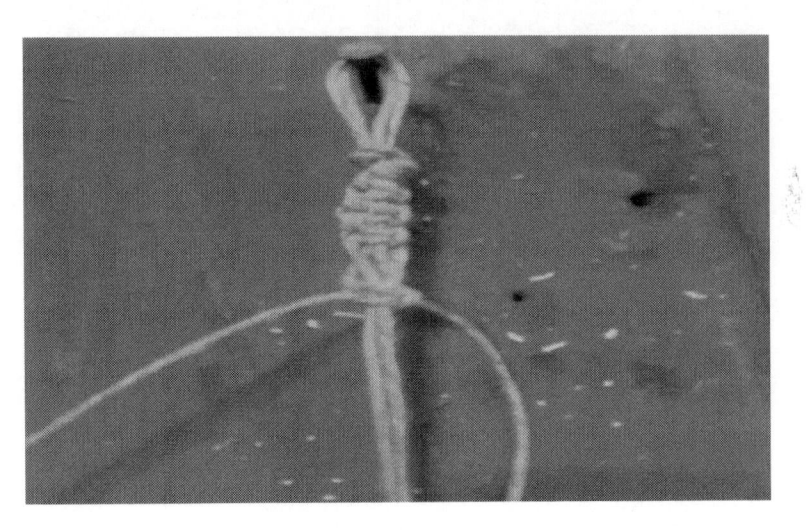

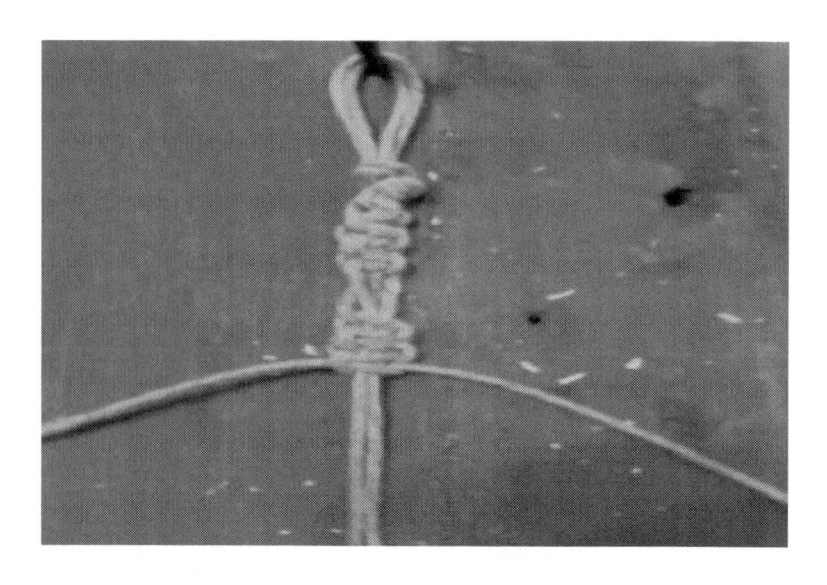

Reverse your strings again and make three more square knots.

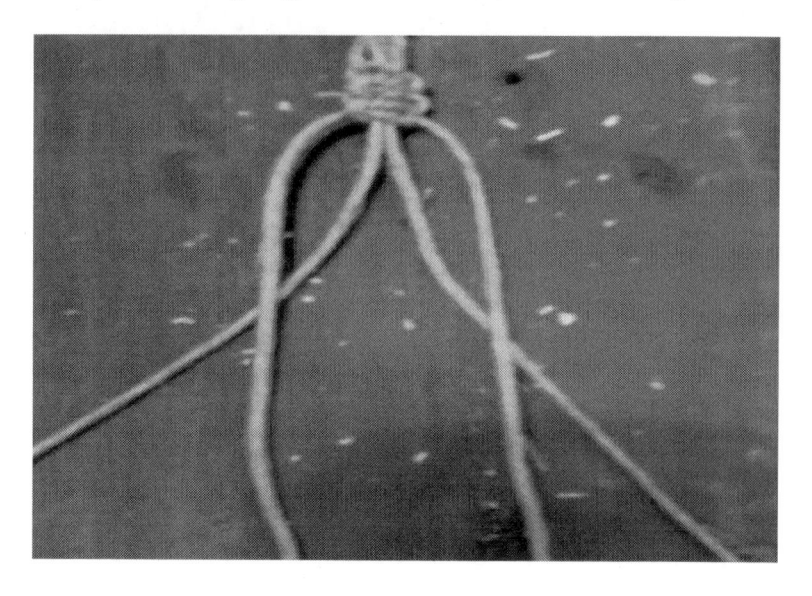

Repeat this pattern for the entire necklace.

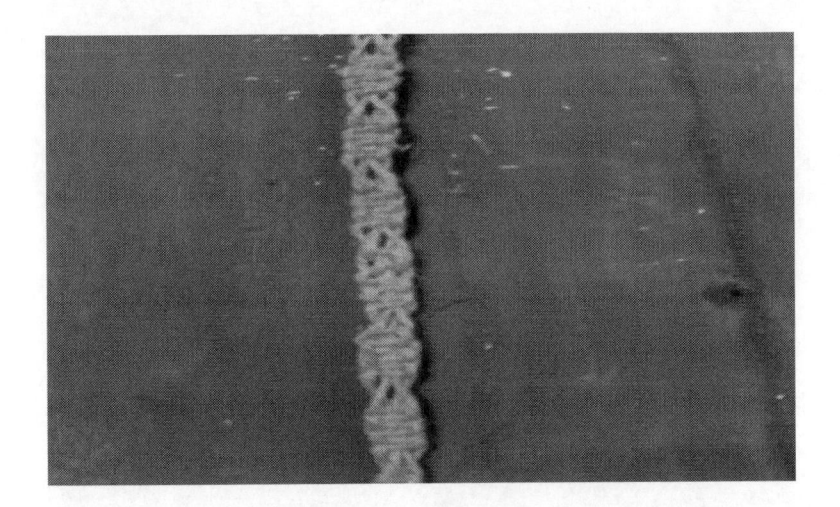

Finish with three square knots and then tie an overhand knot.
Secure with fabric glue.

Square Knot Beaded Anklet

This is a very simple, elegant design. For this anklet I will use four strands. Pull and cut two strands of hemp that are about six times your desired anklet length, plus about one foot. Fold the strands in half and make a loop, secured by an overhand knot.

You should now have four strands. Separate your strands so that you have one strand on either side and two in the middle. You will be making your knots around the two middle strands.

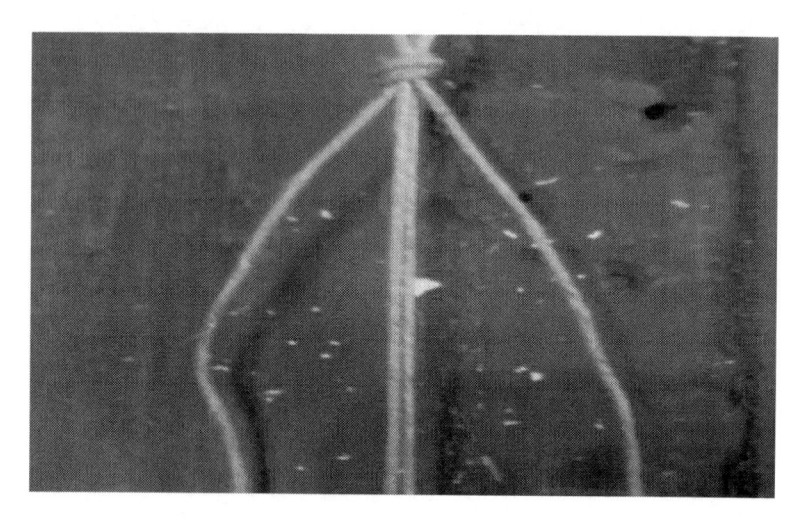

It is easiest to go ahead and string all the beads you will be using at this point. You do not have to be exact. You can always add more or subtract a few if you string too many.

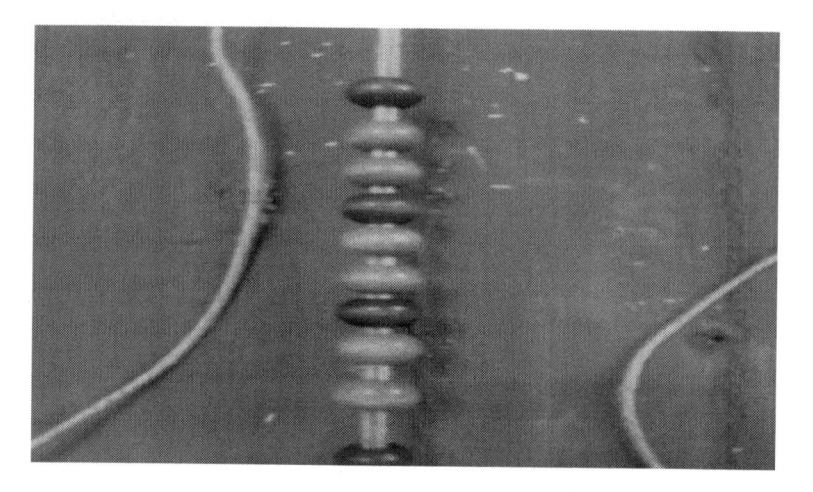

To begin the anklet, make two square knots around the two middle strands using the two outer strands. Move one bead up and make another square knot after it.

Move up your next bead and make another square knot.

Continue the pattern of one bead, then one square knot until you have reached your desired length. End the bracelet with two square knots and an overhand knot. Snip any excess string and secure with fabric glue.

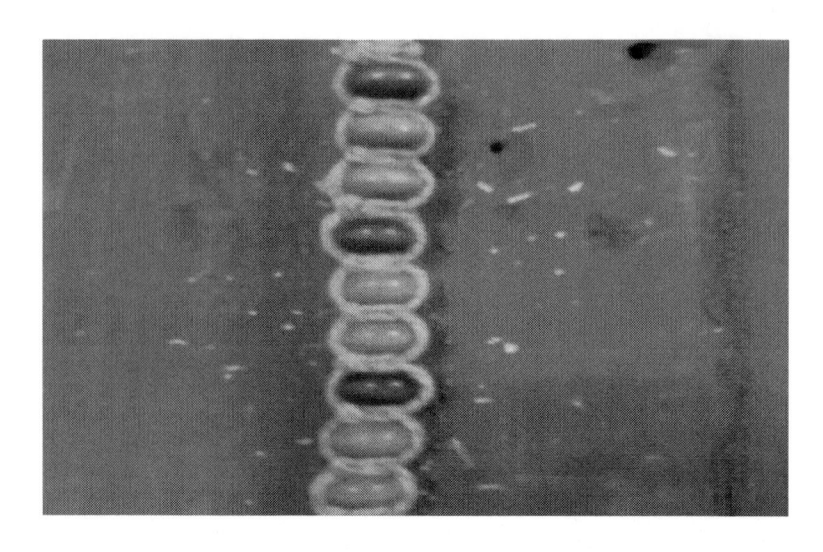

End the anklet with two more square knots.

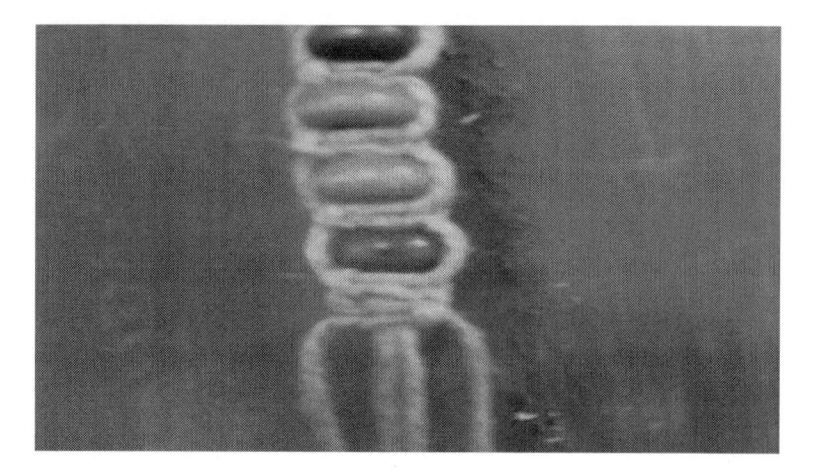

Tie an overhand knot. Tie more than one overhand knot if necessary to add length or to make your knot fit the loop.

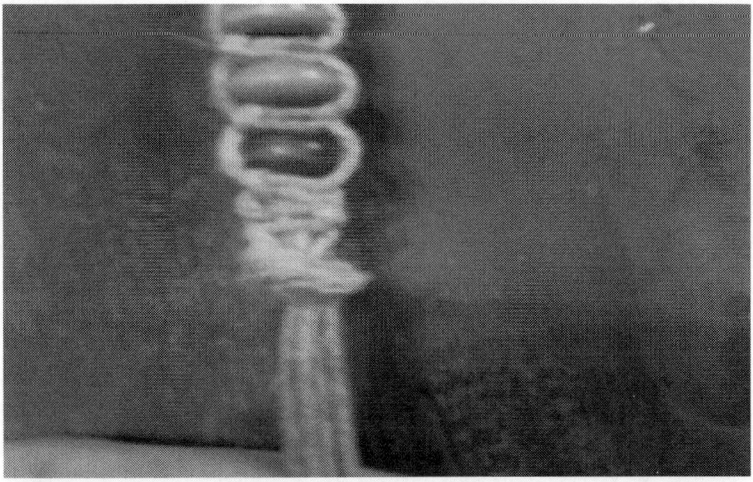

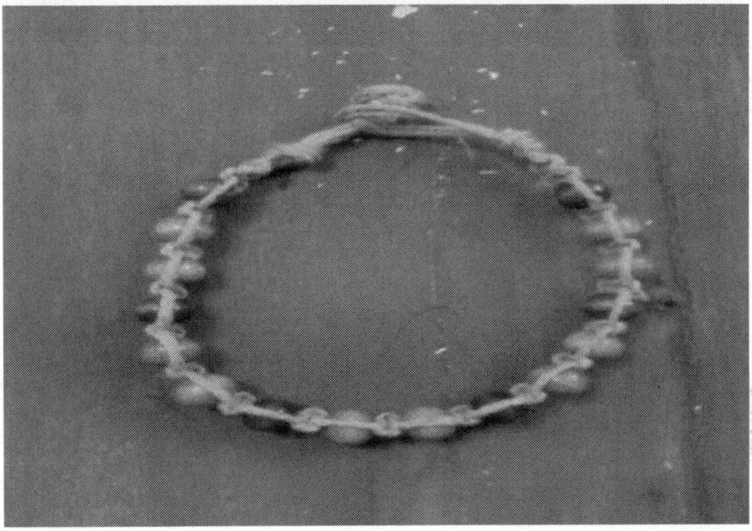

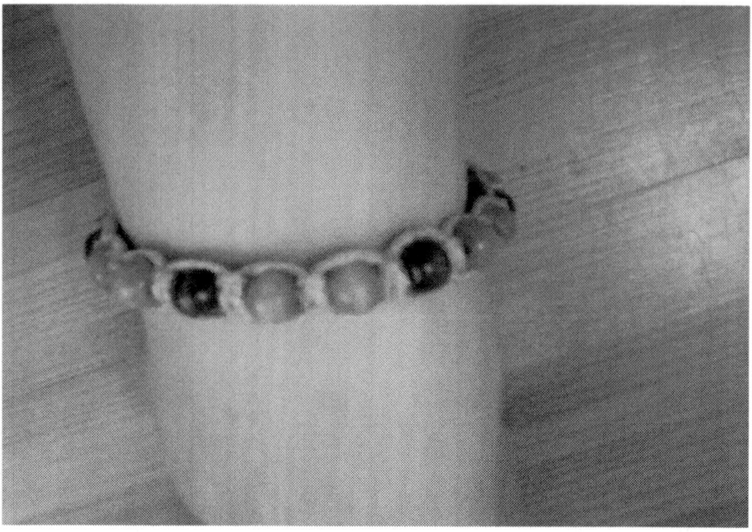

The Half Hitch

The Bar

This style is really good for making belts, though it will require a great deal of patience due to the length you will need. It is very easy to get the long strand tangled.

I will use four strands here. The first strand on the left, which will be used to tie around the other three, needs to be much longer. A good estimate would be about one foot per every inch of length you want in your finished piece. The other three strands can be to scale, or maybe slightly longer just in case. From here I will refer to your long strand as the bar strand to avoid confusion.

From left to right, using your bar strand, tie a half hitch knot in each of the other strands. Here I have knotted the first strand.

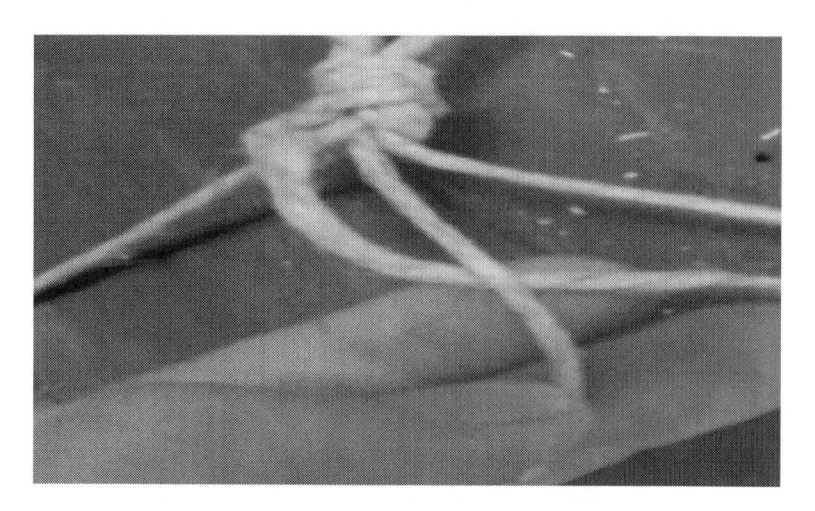

Tie a half hitch knot in the next two strands.

87

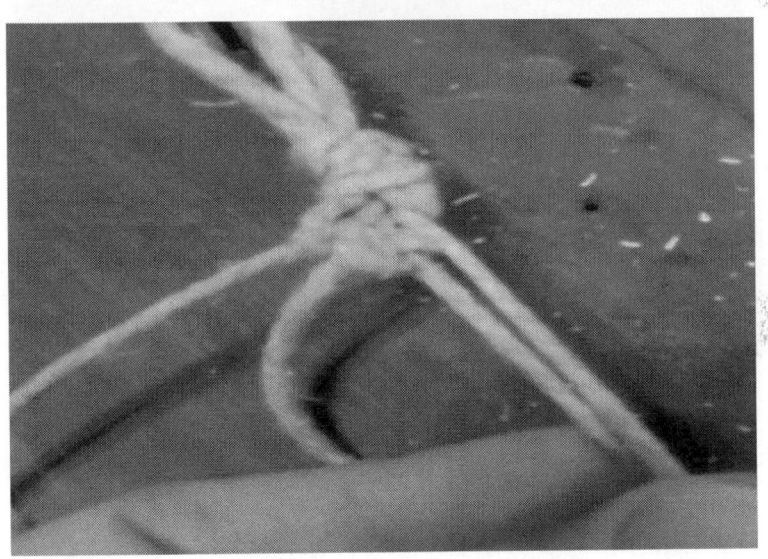

When you have tied a half hitch knot on all three strands, flip your piece over.

Continue tying half hitch knots just as you did the first three. Each time you reach the last strand, flip your piece over and begin a new row of knots, from left to right. In the end, you should have a pattern such as the one shown below:

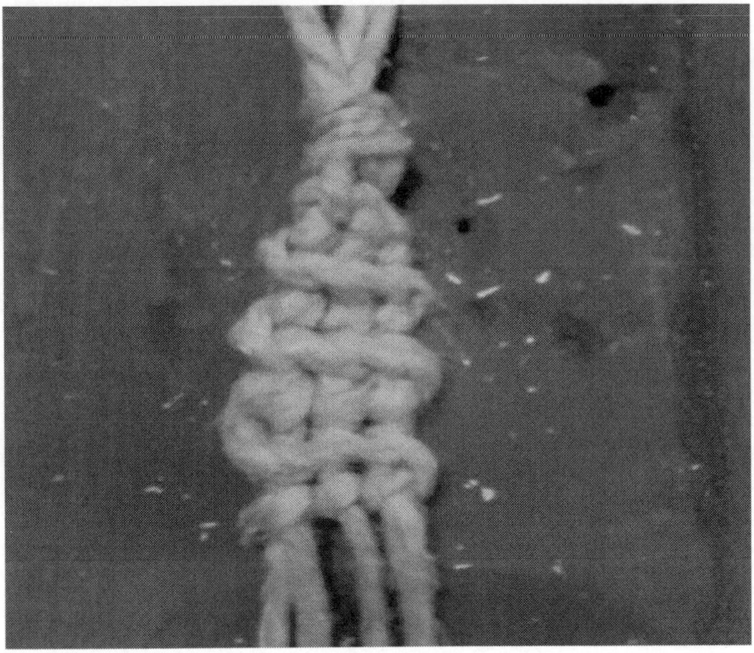

The Overhand Knot

Overhand Knot Belt

Having been a vegetarian for many years, I committed myself to avoiding leather and other animal by-products. Two things that have always been hard (for me) to find are cute non- leather shoes and belts. Aside from the occasional barefoot sandal, I have not yet mastered the shoe part. But I have made quite a few belts which are now an essential part of my wardrobe. The advantage is that I save a lot of money. Not to mention they are personalized to my own taste.

This is a very simple design, but it is tedious, so be prepared to take your time. The end result is well worth it!

Measure around your waist and pull four strands of hemp that are six times that length. Fold all of your strands in half and make an overhand knot.

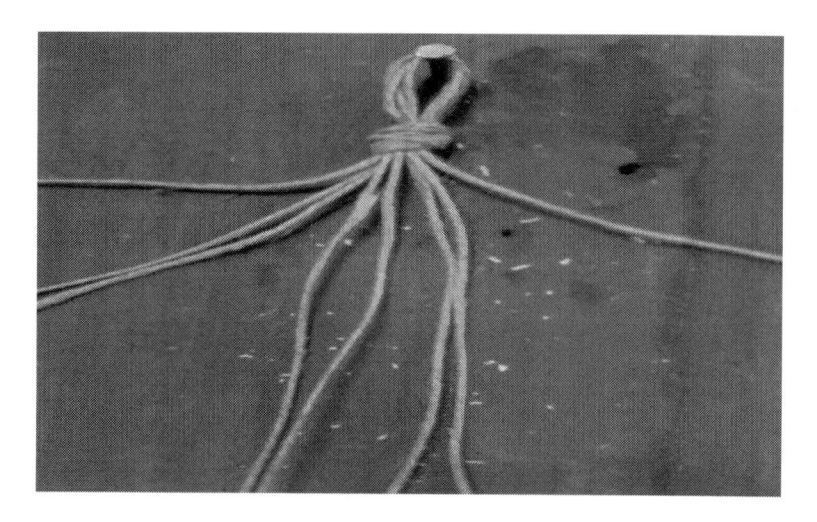

Separate your strands so that you have one strand on either side (you will not use these for knotting in the first row) and three groups of two strands in the middle.

Tie an overhand knot using each group of two strands.

Begin a new row. Separate your strands so that you have four groups of two strands. Tie an overhand knot in each group of two strands.

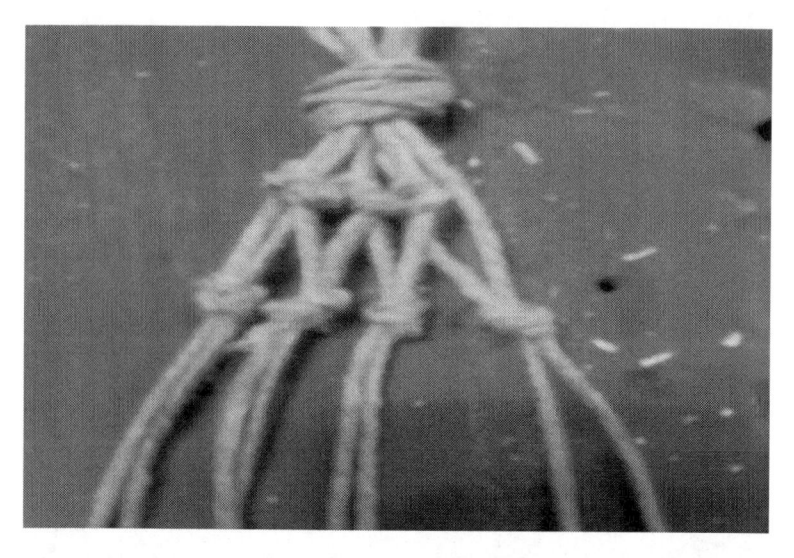

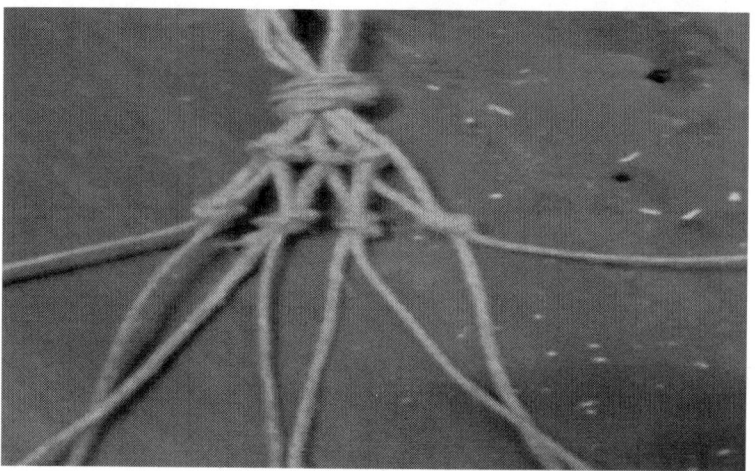

After you have tied overhand knots in all four groups, begin a new row. Separate your strands again so that you have one strand on either side that will not be used for knotting, and three groups of two strands in the middle, just as you did to begin the belt.

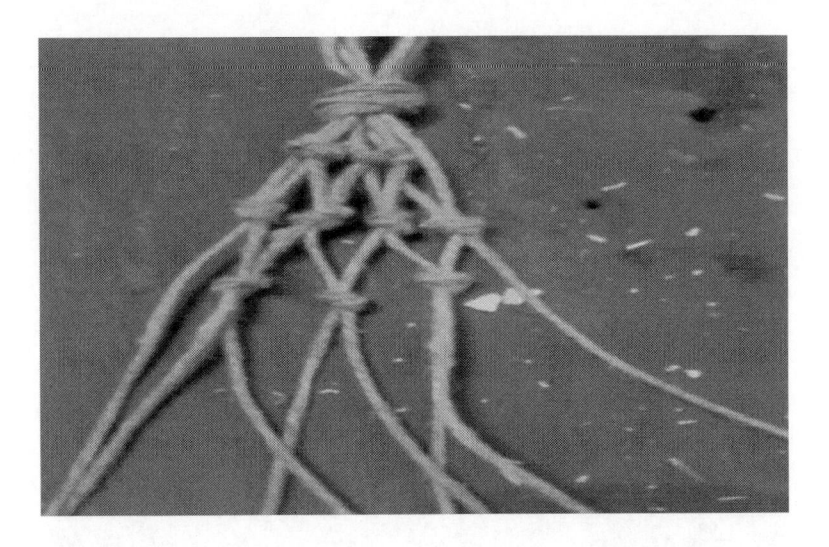

Tie overhand knots in each of the three groups of two strands.

Repeat the pattern of three knots, then four knots, then three knots again until you achieve your desired length for the belt. You should end up with a design that resembles the one shown above.

At the end of my belts, I like to leave "fringe". I think it adds a very pretty, chic element. Plus, it gives me a little room to grow. Not that I have ever needed it. Ahem, so anyways....

There are several creative ways to end this belt. I will give a few options below.

Option one: Simply tie an overhand knot. Use the hanging fringe through your loop to tie the belt.

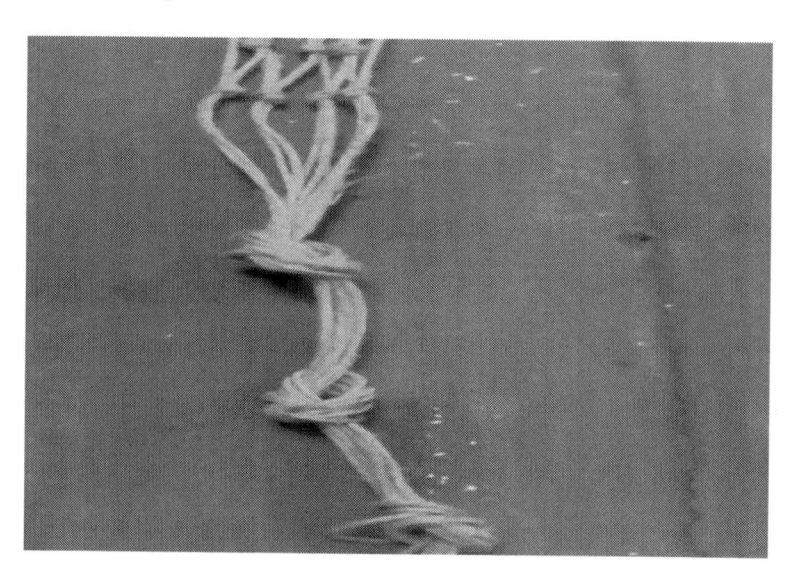

Option two: Tie several overhand knots as shown above. This is still cute, but you will have less fringe.

Option three: End with a bead and one overhand knot as shown above. It will add a decorative element and you will still have fringe.

Option four: End with several beads and secure each bead with overhand knots on either side, as shown in the picture above. You could even add two or three beads between knots. You might even opt to tie several smaller beads on each strand so that you can keep the fringe and still have beads for more decoration. The possibilities are endless.

Chapter Review:

- Use waxed hemp for the fishbone design if you have it available.
- Do not get your fishbone design wet.
- With one type of knot, you can make several different styles.
- Be sure to allow adequate room at the end of your jewelry to make closing knots.
- You can make clothing accessories as well as making jewelry.

Chapter 4: How to Braid

Up to this point in the guide, I have focused mainly on making jewelry with different knots. However, there are ways to make hemp jewelry without using knots, for the most part, at least. This chapter will center on other ways to make hemp jewelry, such as weaving and braiding. These styles are incredibly simple to make, and they produce fantastic jewelry to boot.

Braiding

This style is extremely easy and takes very little time. If you have ever braided hair, the method is much the same. As you braid, keep an eye on the other end of your strands so that they remain separated. Otherwise, they will begin to braid as well, in the opposite direction. It can be a real pain to unbraid them if you have been braiding for a while. Plus, when you have to stop and untangle them, the braid you have been working on tends to become loose.

I will be using three strands in this example. To start, cut a strand about six inches or so more than your desired length. Then cut another strand twice that length. Fold the longer strand in half and make a loop. Tie an overhand knot at one end of the shorter strand if desired. Place the knotted end of the shorter strand inside the loop and tie an overhand knot using all of the strands to secure the loop and the extra strand.

Note: I will be braiding very loosely here so that it is easy to see the strands as they cross over one another. You would normally want to keep your braid tighter.

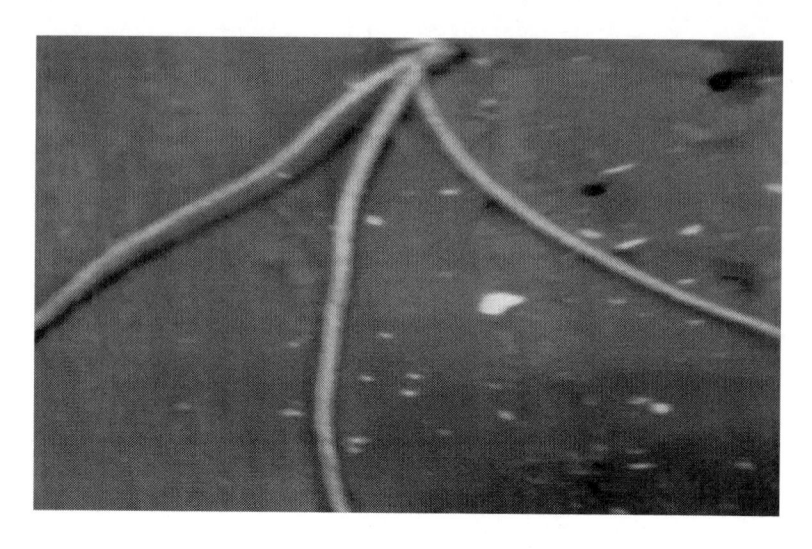

Grasp the outermost strand on the right. Cross it over the middle strand.

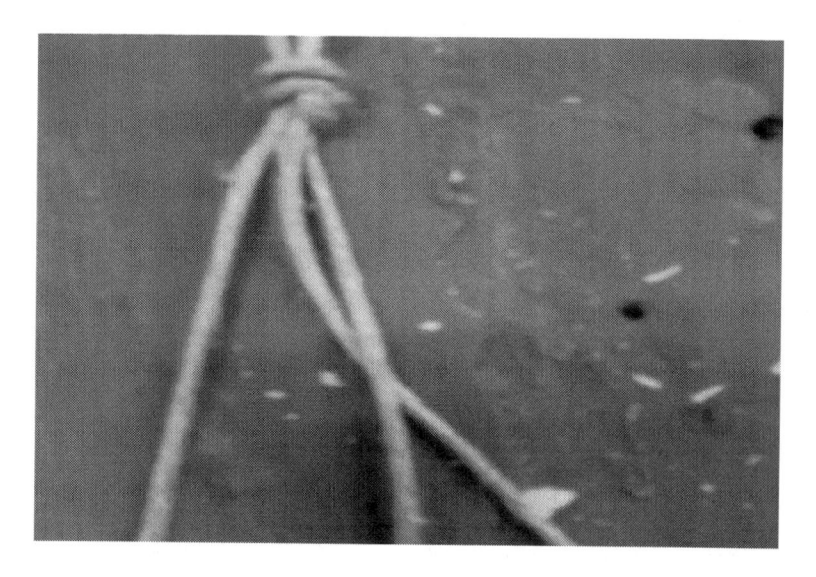

Now grasp the outermost strand on the left. Cross it over the strand that was on the right, but is now the middle strand.

Now grab the outermost strand on the right and repeat the process from the beginning, always alternating right and left.

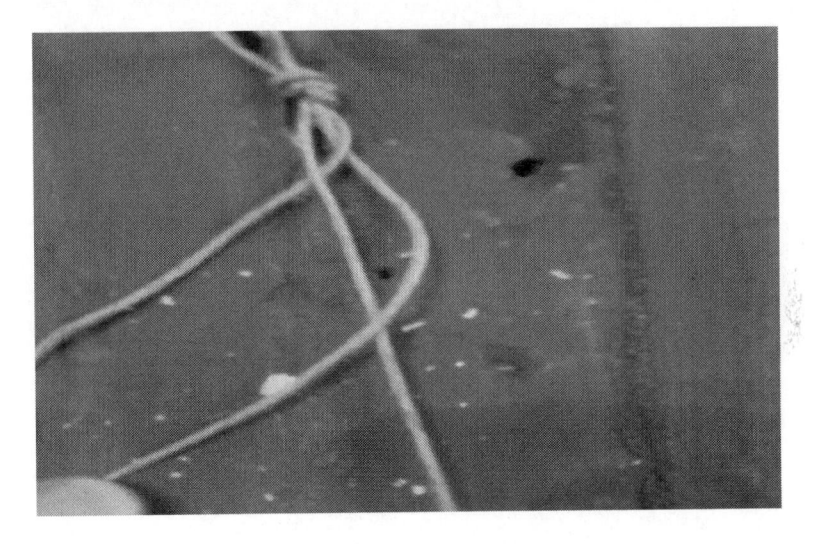

You should end up with a pattern like the one shown below:

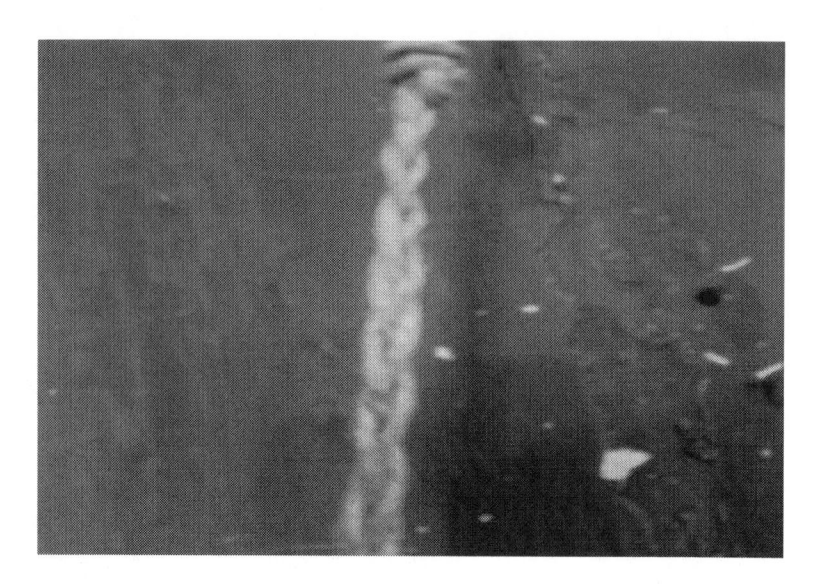

If you would like to add beads, simply string your bead(s) onto whatever the middle strand is at the time and continue to braid. You can also just string beads over the finished braid, or create an interesting pattern using both ideas.

How to Weave

For weaving, I will use two examples. For the first I will use five strands. For the second example I will use seven strands. I recommend thinner hemp for this style of jewelry, as it will be easier to work with. If you do use thicker hemp, be sure to increase the length of the strands you are using.

Five Strand Woven Band Bracelet

Cut two strands of hemp. For this bracelet you will probably need about two feet in length for two of the strands. Your weaver strand will need to be around five feet.

Tie an overhand knot on one end of your weaver strand (optional). Fold your two foot strands in half, making a loop in the center. Place the knotted end of your weaver strand in the center of the loop. Tie an overhand knot to secure your weaver string and loop.

Separate your strands so that your weaver strand is the outermost strand to your left. Separate the other strands into two sets of two. The weaver strand in this example is orange.

Bring your weaver strand underneath the first set of two strands and over the second set, as shown above.

Now bring your weaver strand underneath the second set of strands and over the first.

Repeat this pattern the opposite way. Bring your weaver strand underneath the two strands on the left and over the two strands on the right. Repeat again the opposite way, going under then over.

When repeated, you should have a pattern resembling the one shown above.

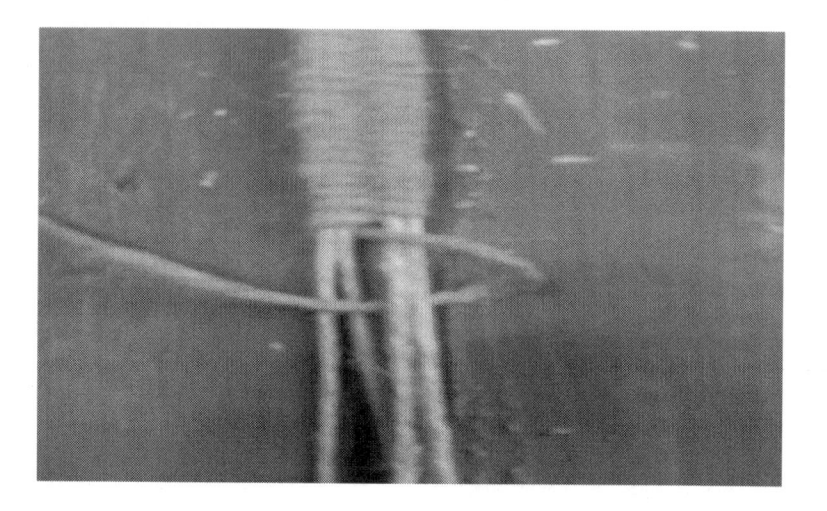

Continue this pattern through the length of your bracelet. When you reach your desired length, tie a half hitch knot to end your weaving, as shown in the picture below.

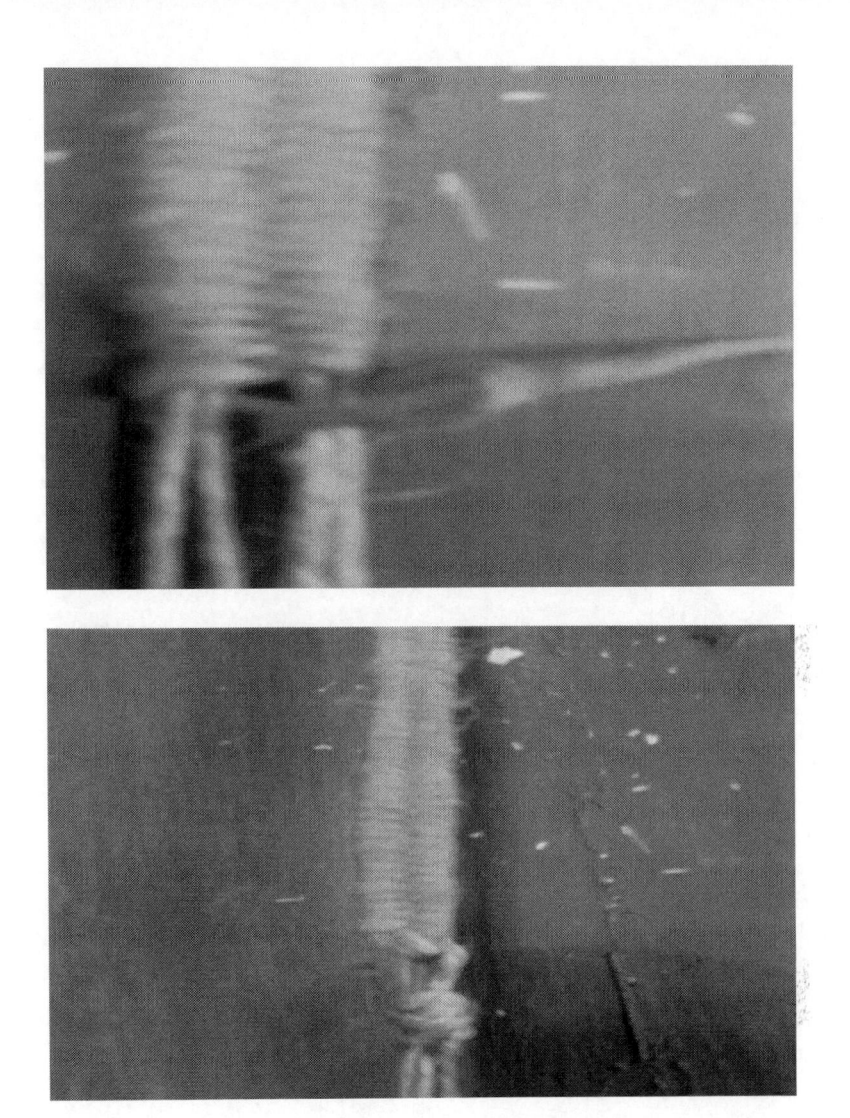

To end your bracelet, tie a half twist or square knot. Then tie an overhand knot, trim any excess strands and secure your overhand knot with fabric glue.

Seven Strand Woven Band Bracelet

Cut three strands of hemp around two feet long each. This time you will need around seven to eight feet in length for your weaver strand, or a little longer if you are using thick hemp.

Begin this bracelet exactly the way you did the five strand woven band bracelet. When you have secured your loop and weaver strand, separate your strands so that the weaver strand is the outermost strand to your left. The weaver strand in this example is yellow.

Separate the rest of the strands into three sets of two.

The weaving for this bracelet begins a little differently than in the five strand bracelet, but aside from that, the process is the same. Pull your weaver strand between the two strands in the first set to your left.

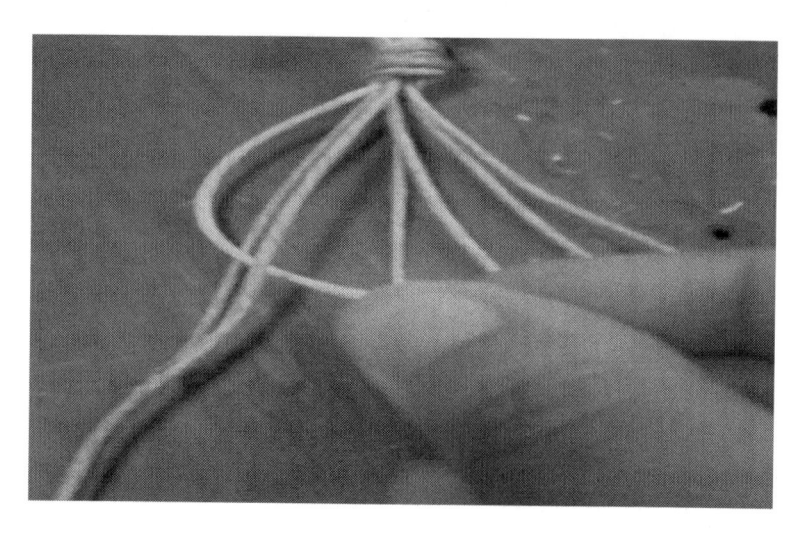

Bring the weaver strand over the next set of two strands and under the last set of two.

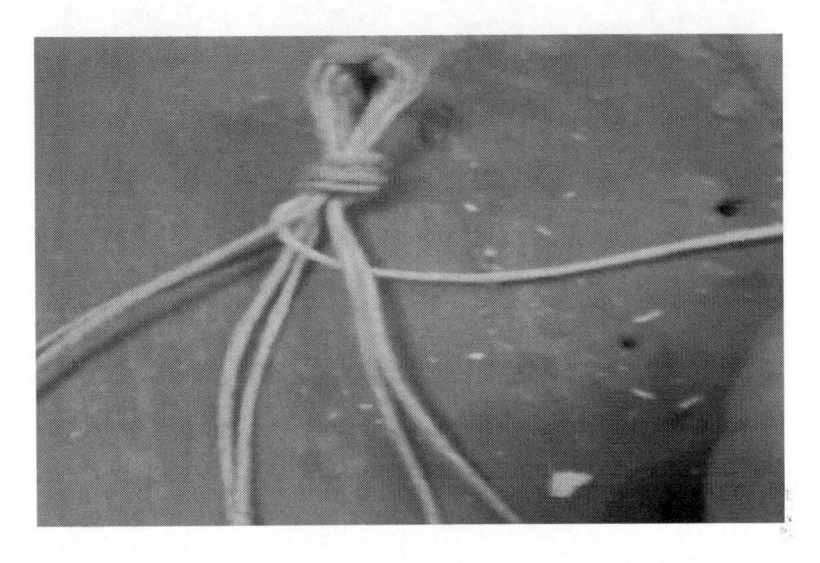

Bring your weaver strand back over the last set of two strands going the opposite direction, as shown below.

Now take your weaver strand underneath the middle set of two strands and over the last set.

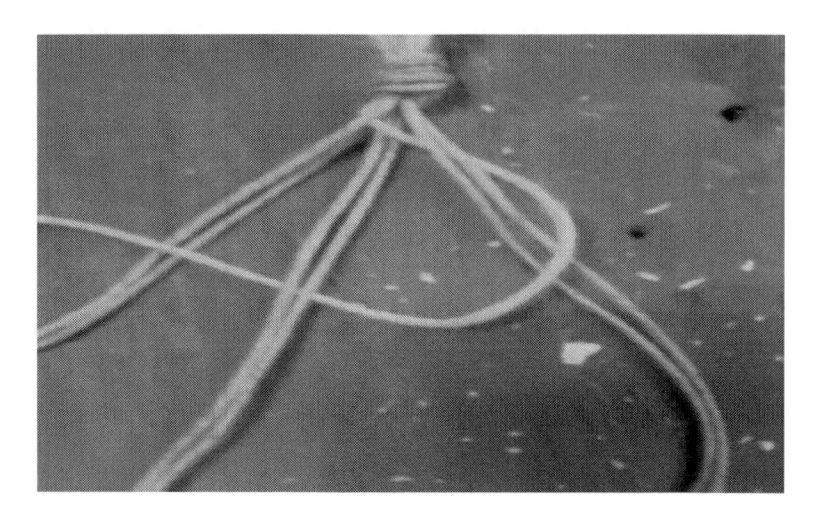

Now bring your weaver strand underneath the last set of strands and over the middle set.

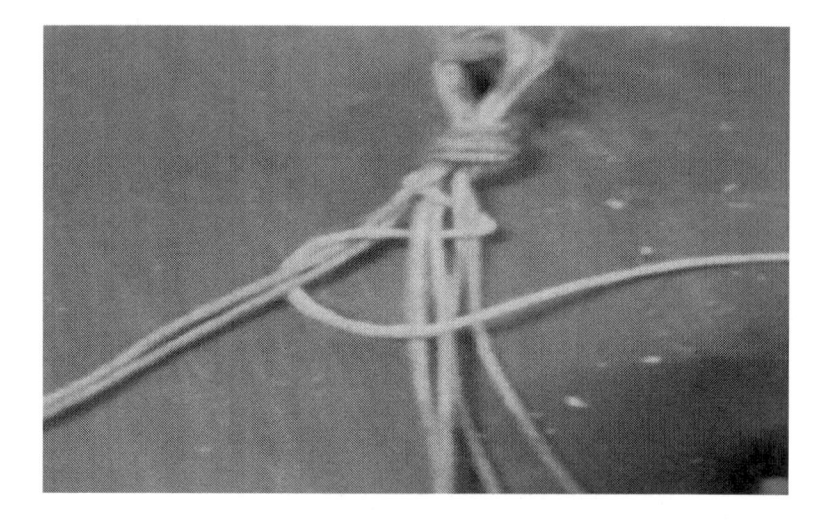

Continue the pattern of over and under each set until you reach your desired bracelet length.

When you reach your desired length, tie an overhand knot in the center set of two strands with your weaver strand.

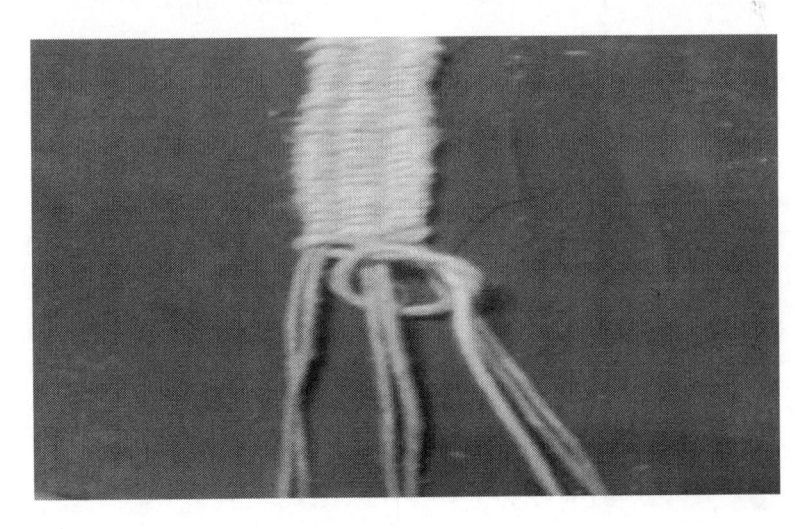

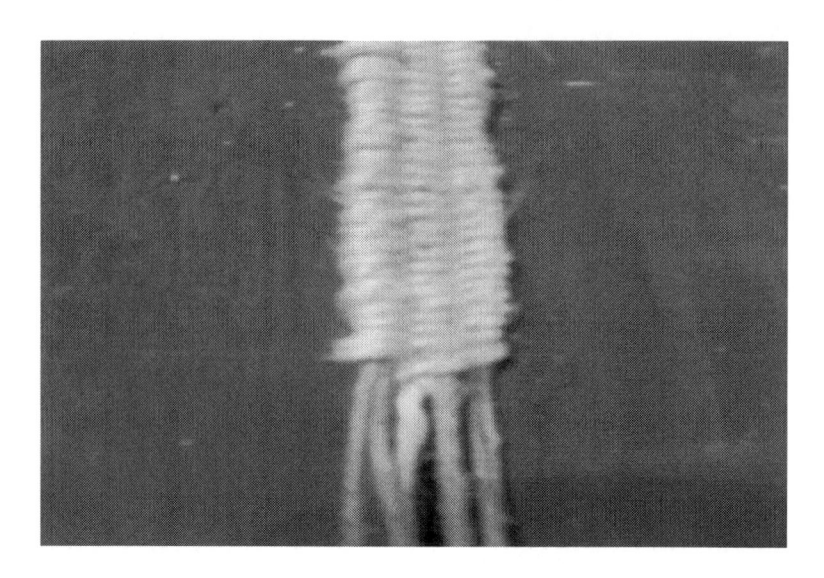

End your bracelet with an overhand knot. Snip any excess material and secure your overhand knot with fabric glue.

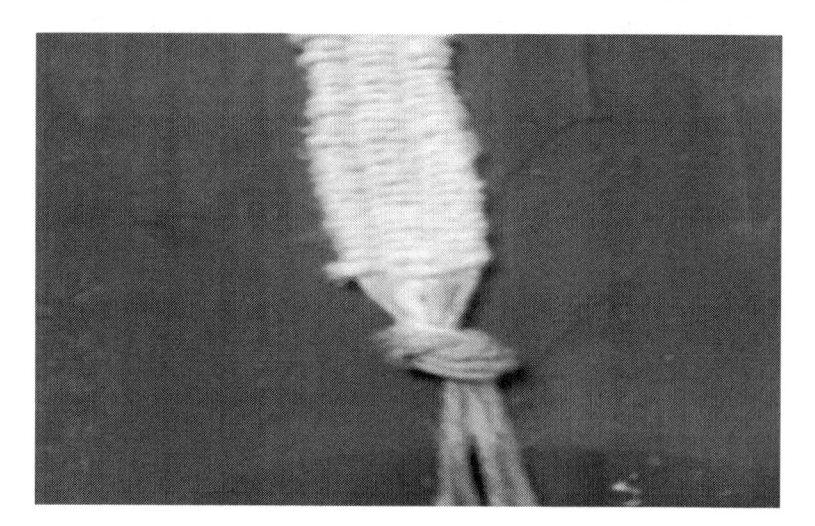

Chapter Review

- You can make beautiful hemp jewelry without using knots.
- Braiding is extremely simple. Plus, you do not need a lot of extra length when braiding. Your strands can be almost to scale.
- When weaving, your weaver strand will need to be much longer than your other strands.

- A good rule of thumb is for every foot, you will need an additional one and a half to two feet additional length for your weaver strand.
- Keep in mind, when weaving, that your weaver strand will need more length as you add more strands to your pattern as well.

Chapter 5: Mix It Up

In this chapter you will find creative ideas for pendant and beaded jewelry using the techniques demonstrated in the previous chapters. I will provide step by step instructions for each jewelry piece. Happy hemping!

Pendant Jewelry

You can always string a pendant onto your jewelry as you go (I will provide an example of this), just like another bead, or with jump rings. Or you can begin with your pendant and work your way out. This chapter will show several styles of pendant jewelry that you can make.

Simple Overhand Knot Pendant Necklace

This design is both simple and elegant. You will only need a few minutes to make this dainty necklace.

For this necklace, I will use four strands.

Cut two strands of hemp about six inches to one foot longer than the desired length of your necklace. Position your pendant in the very center of the two strands.

Tie an overhand knot to secure the pendant. You could add a bead over the overhand knot and tie another overhand knot at this point if you would like. Just an idea.

Separate your strands so that you have two strands on the right and two strands on the left. About one inch from the overhand knot you used to secure your pendant (or extra bead), tie an overhand knot on each side.

Continue tying overhand knots using one inch spacing throughout the rest of the necklace.

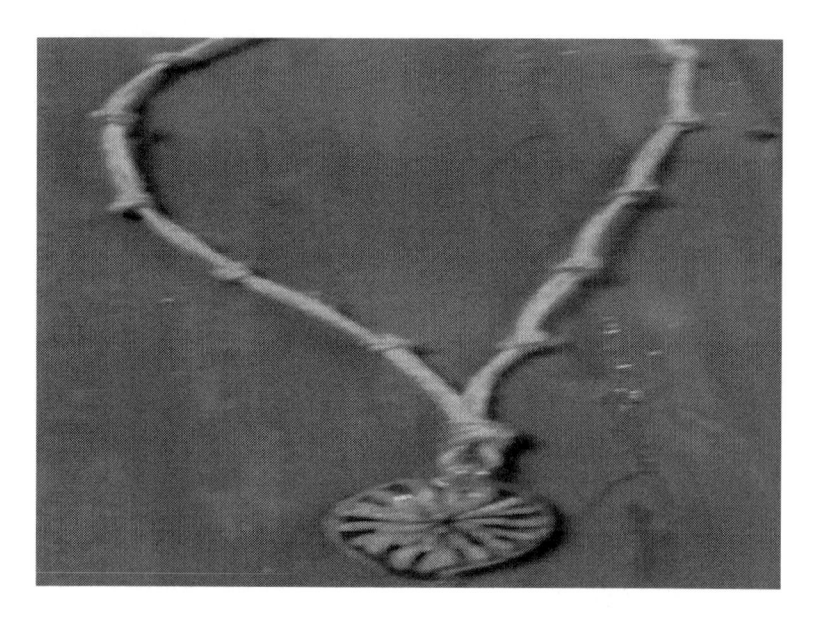

To end, tie an overhand knot using all of your strings. If your necklace is not long enough to slip over your head, you may opt to tie an overhand knot on each side. That way you can take it off and put it on by tying and untying a simple knot when you wear it.

Alternatively, you can make adjustable knots with beads to eliminate the trouble of tying and untying knots every time you put on or take off your necklace. Here is how to do it:

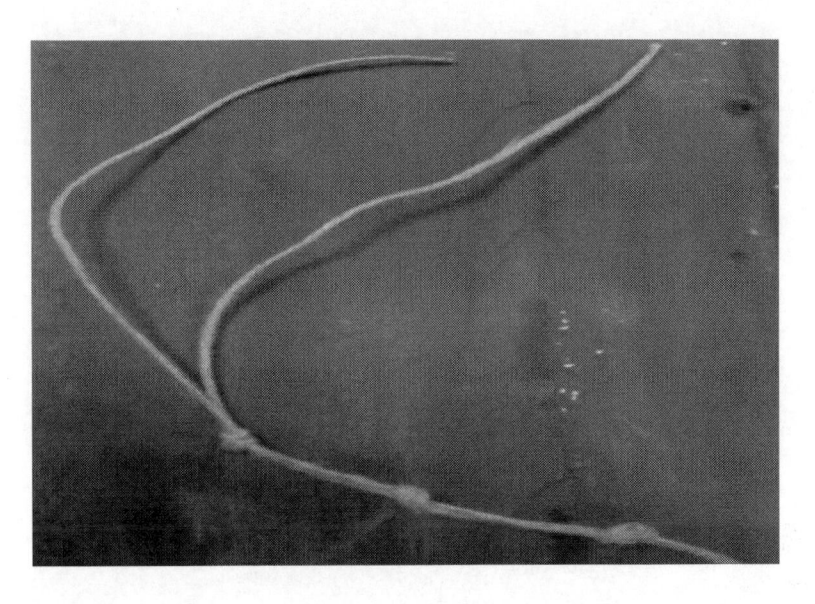

Taking one side of your necklace, thread your strands through a bead. Be sure that the ends of the strands are going through the bead in opposite directions.

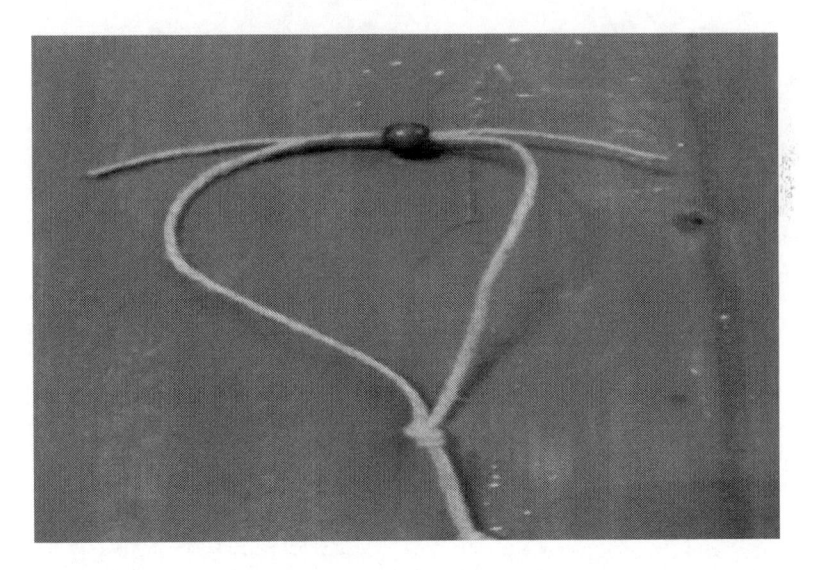

Tie a couple of regular knots to secure the bead. Leave four to six inches from your last overhand knot and where you tie your bead.

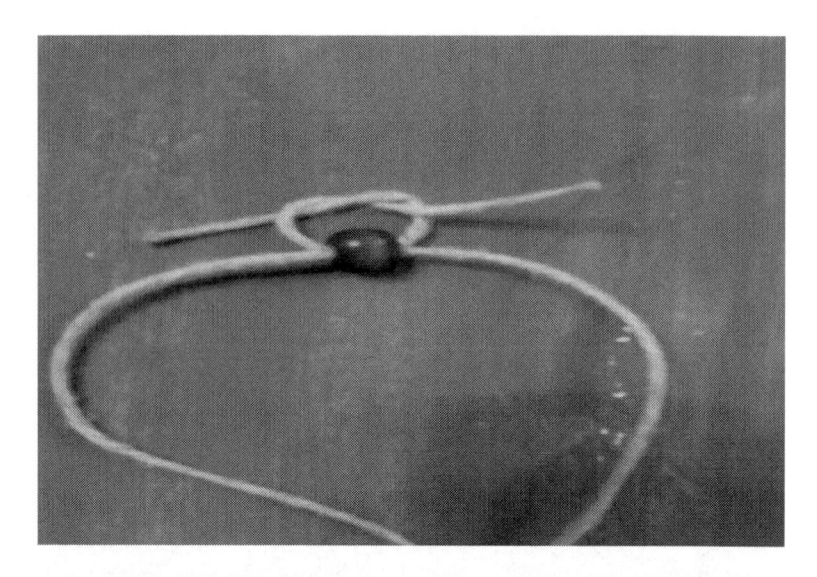

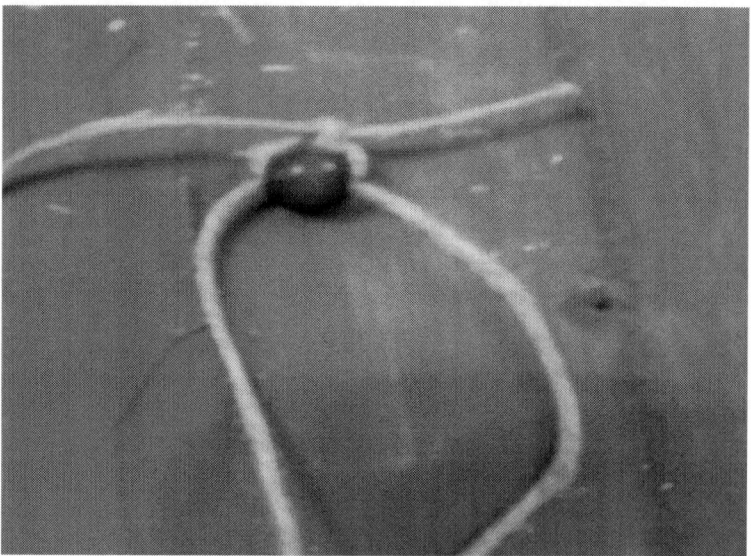

Grip the knot abovethe bead and pull down on the bead. This will create a loop like the one shown below. Now repeat this entire process on the other side of your necklace. Cut away the excess hemp strand and secure the knots with fabric glue. In this case, fabric glue is necessary to keep your knots from coming undone.

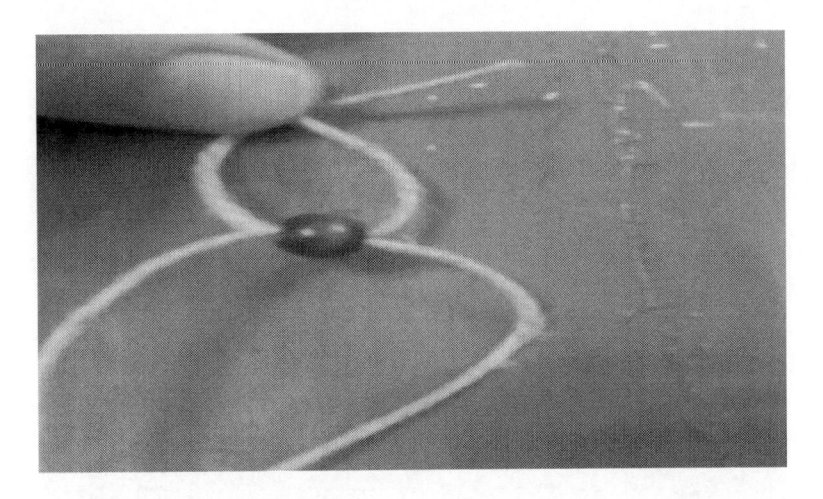

After the fabric glue has dried, push one bead back up to the knot. Thread the bead through the loop above the second bead on the other side.

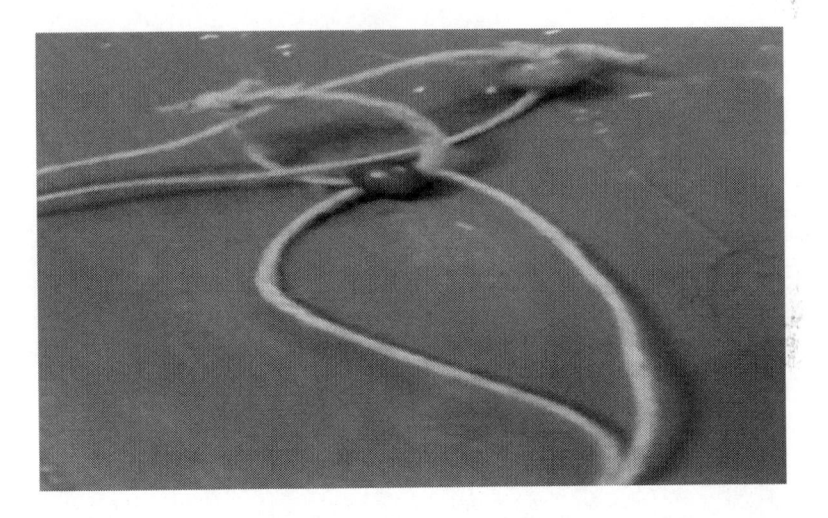

Now push the second bead up to close the loop around the first bead.

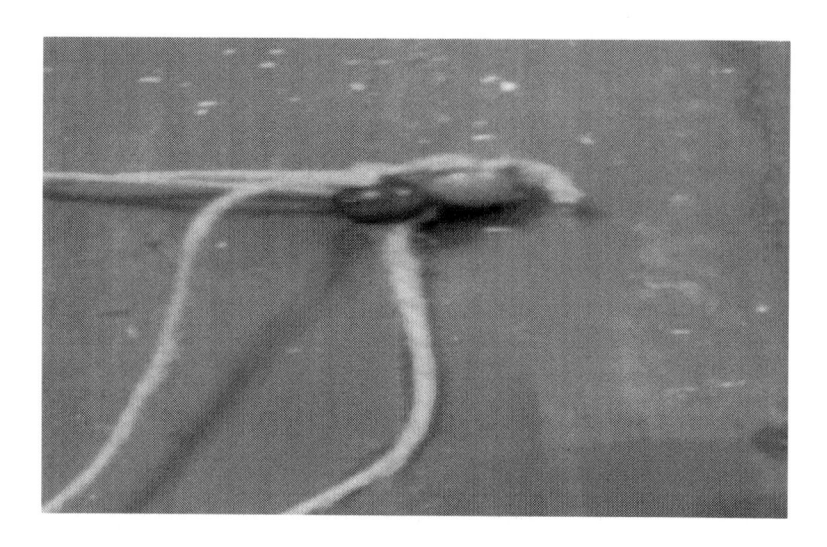

You can close your loops at different points in your strands for an adjustable necklace.

Other ways to end this necklace: Tie one or two beads on each side for fashionable flair. You can tie an overhand knot before and after the beads to secure them. Tie the necklace to wear it, just as you would if you had tied an overhand knot on either side.

Simple Overhand Knot Pendant Necklace Variation With Beads

Cut two strands of hemp as you did in the first example of the simple overhand knot pendant necklace. String your pendant to the center of your strands and secure with an overhand knot.

Separate your strands into two groups of two. Tie an overhand knot on each side, one inch from the overhand knot used to secure your pendant. String a bead on each side and tie another overhand knot.

Skip another inch and tie an overhand knot on each side. String and secure another bead.

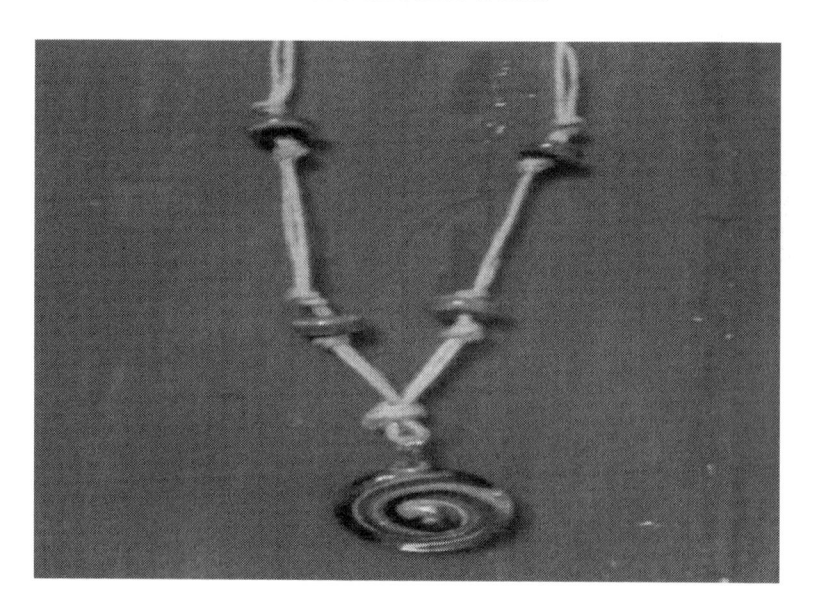

Continue this pattern for the entire length of the necklace. End the necklace by tying two overhand knots, stringing beads and making loops, or tying a single overhand knot, just as is shown in the first example of this necklace.

Alternate ending for this necklace: This ending will only work if the necklace is long enough to slip over your head. Leave about six to eight inches from your last overhand knots to the ending of your necklace. On either side, tie overhand knots toward the end of your strands. String a bead on each side and tie overhand knots to secure the beads.

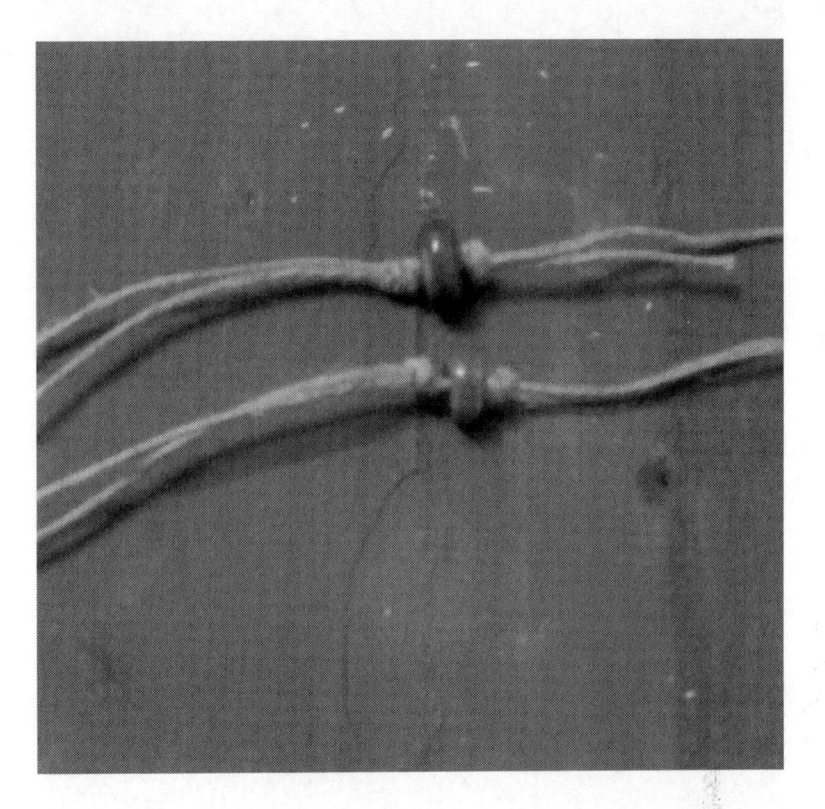

Place the end of each strand of your necklace so that they are one atop the other, and facing opposite directions.

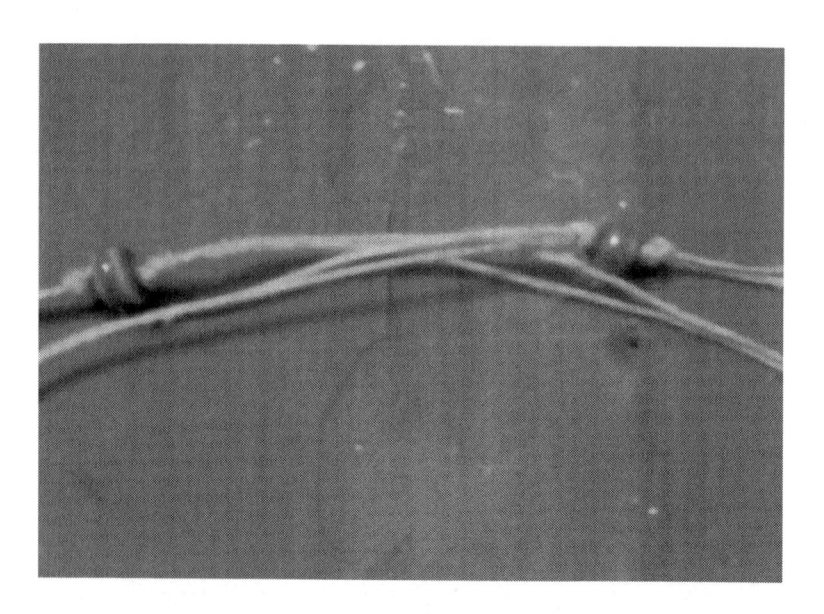

Cut a separate strand of hemp that is around one foot in length. Using this strand, tie a regular knot around the two overlapping sets of strands at the end of your necklace.

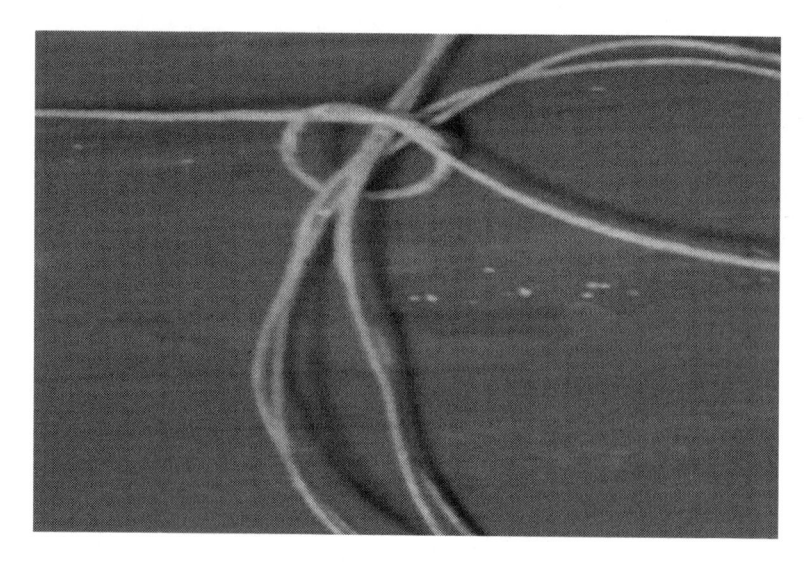

Tie six square knots around the other strands using your one foot long piece you used to tie the ends together. Then tie an overhand knot in both strands after you have tied your square knots. Cut away excess hemp and secure with fabric glue. Be sure not to get any glue on the necklace strands.

123

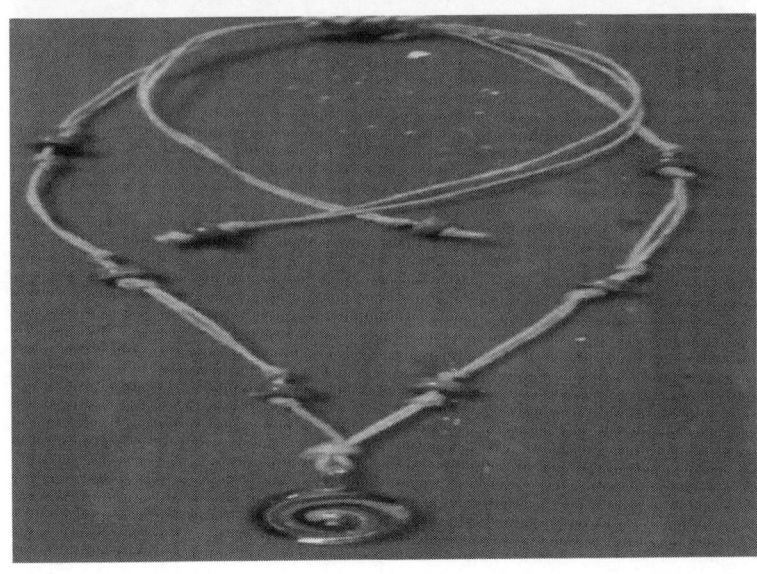

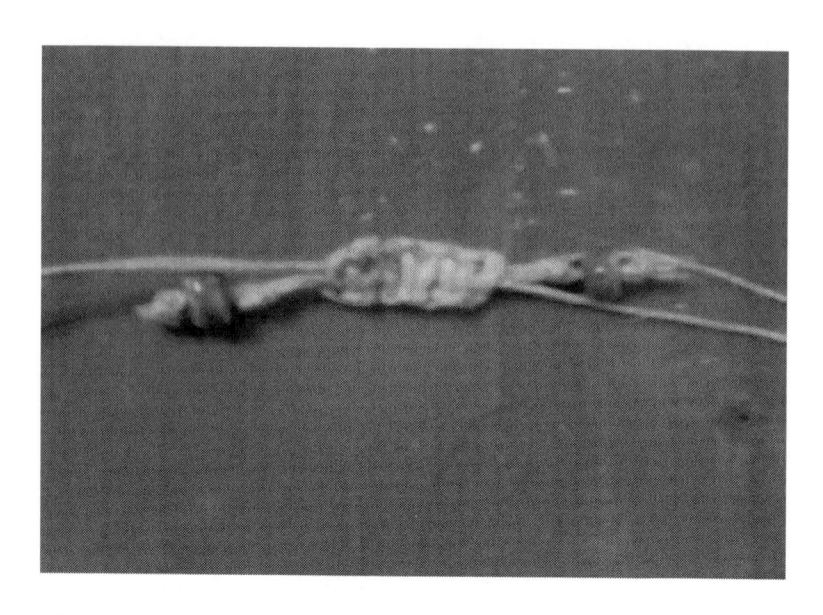

The necklace strands will slide through your square knot closure, making your jewelry adjustable.

Alternating Half Hitch Pendant Necklace

Cut two strands of hemp about eight feet long. Cut one strand about four feet. Fold your eight foot strand in half, making a loop, and place your four foot strand inside the loop. Secure your loop with an overhand knot.

Begin making alternating half hitch knots until you reach half your desired length. Tie an overhand knot at the mid-point of your necklace and string your pendant.

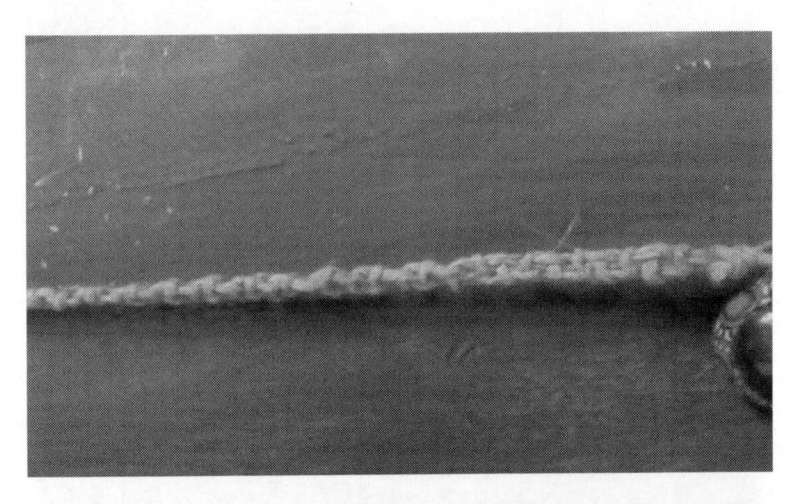

Tie another overhand knot on the other side of your pendant. Continue making alternating half hitch knots.

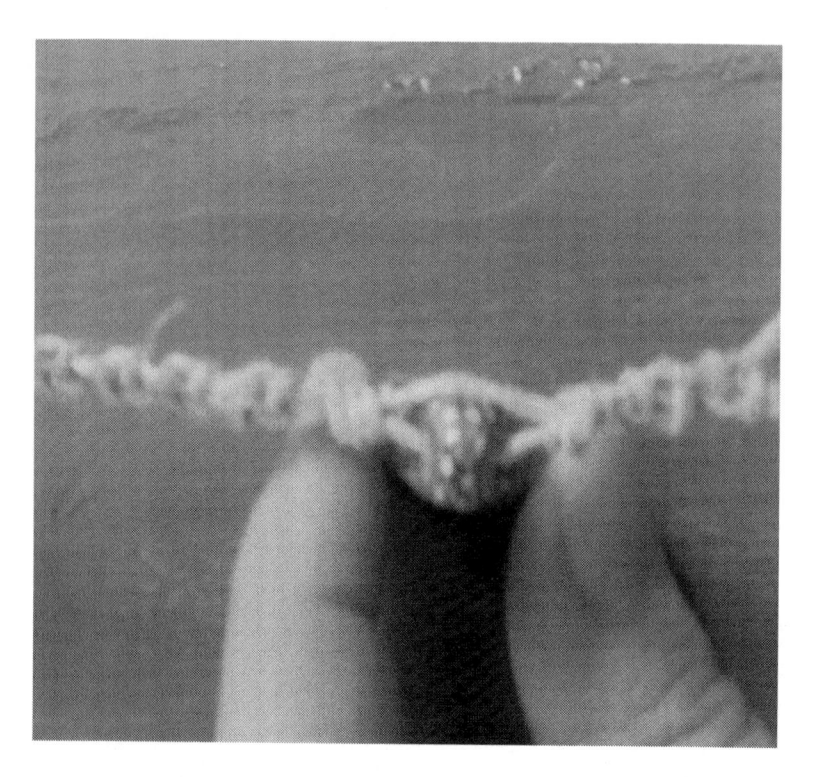

String your pendant over all of your strands if it will fit. If not, you can string it over one or two strands, then tuck the other strand or strands behind your pendant.

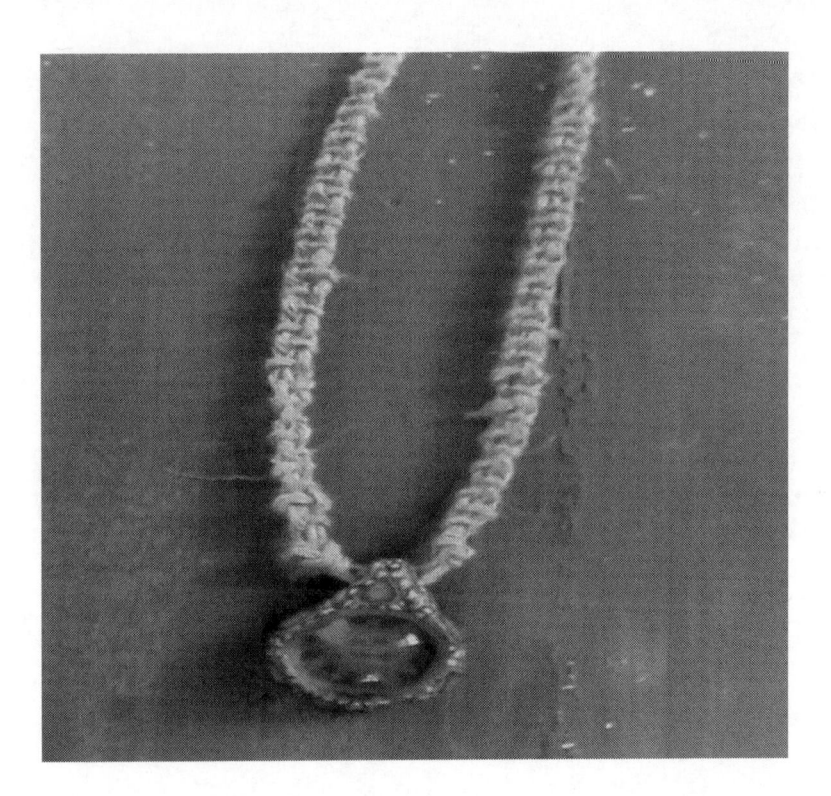

End the necklace with an overhand knot. Snip away any excess cord and secure your overhand knot with fabric glue.

Ways That You Can Make Your Jewelry Adjustable

When I began making jewelry, the only closure I knew how to make was the loop and knot closure. Eventually, I wanted to learn other ways to finish my jewelry. The finish is just as important as the rest of the piece, so I will use this section of the guide to suggest several options for you to finish your jewelry.

The loop and knot closure is very simple and does the job, but one advantage it does not have is adjustability. When making jewelry for yourself, you will know exactly what size you need. However, it is not so simple when making jewelry for others. If you are unsure of what size you need, it is a good idea to make your piece adjustable. Here I will give examples on how to make your jewelry adaptable to the needs of others. You can always use chain with clasps at the end of your jewelry to make it adjustable. However, you will have to go and purchase these things. I think you can make very professional looking adjustable jewelry without having to spend the extra money, and using only hemp fiber to do it.

Adjustable jewelry has a much neater look than the loop and knot closure. The loop and knot is great for long necklaces and for chokers, but sometimes feels bulky for anklets or bracelets or other small jewelry.

I have given examples of some of these different closures previously in this guide. Here, I will go over them again using the minimal amount of strands so that it is easier to see what I am doing. I suggest practicing each method. Use scrap hemp if you have any available. If not, use strands that are about a foot or less in length.

Braid Closure

A very simple way to make your jewelry adjustable is to begin and end with a length of braid. This gives the person wearing the jewelry an option to tie the jewelry tightly, or to wear it loosely.

To begin your jewelry, determine the length you want for your braid. Keep in mind that it will be used for tying, so you probably want to make it at least six inches.

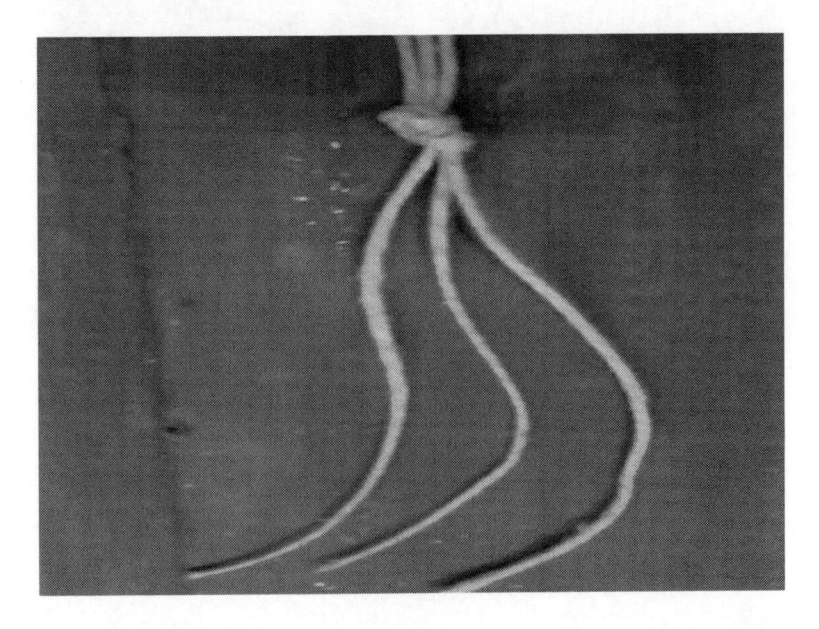

Six or so inches from the end, tie an overhand knot. Braid from that overhand knot back down, and then tie another overhand knot at the end.

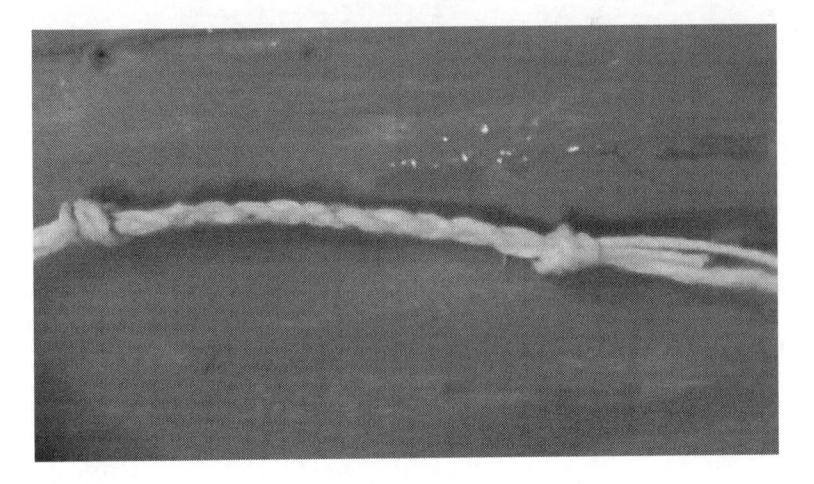

Starting on the other side of the first overhand knot you made six inches in, begin your pattern for your jewelry.

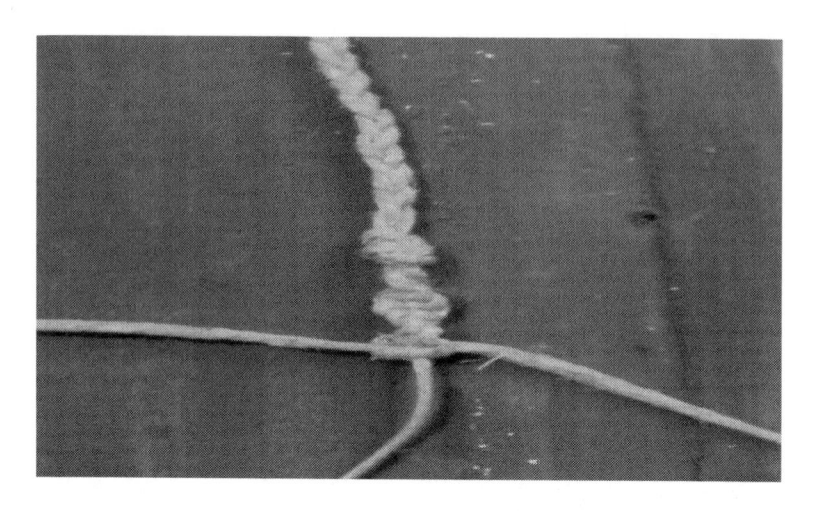

When you have achieved your desired length, tie another overhand knot.

Braid again for the length you did at the beginning (six or so inches) and tie another overhand knot. Snip excess material and secure each end with fabric glue. Now you have an adjustable piece of jewelry!

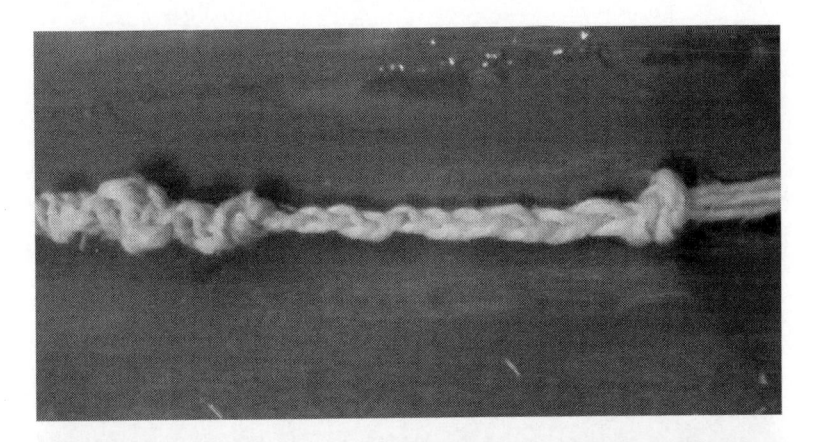

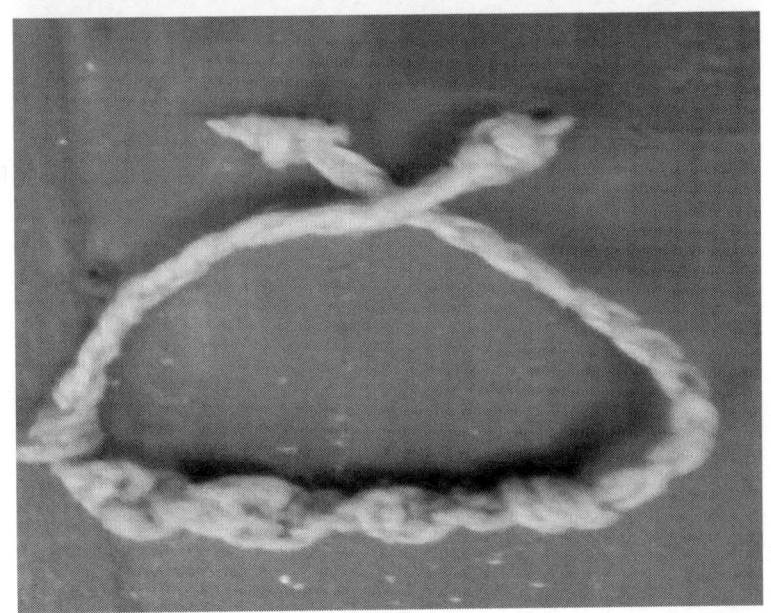

Square Knot Closure

For this example I will use two strands that are about one and a half feet in length. This is practice, so length is not important here. If you have somewhat long scrap pieces, this would be a great time to use them.

I have made overhand knots at each end of the first strand to keep the strands from sliding through the closure. Making the knots also makes it easier to see where to start the closure.

Lay the ends of your jewelry piece one on top of another, facing opposite directions, as shown in the picture below.

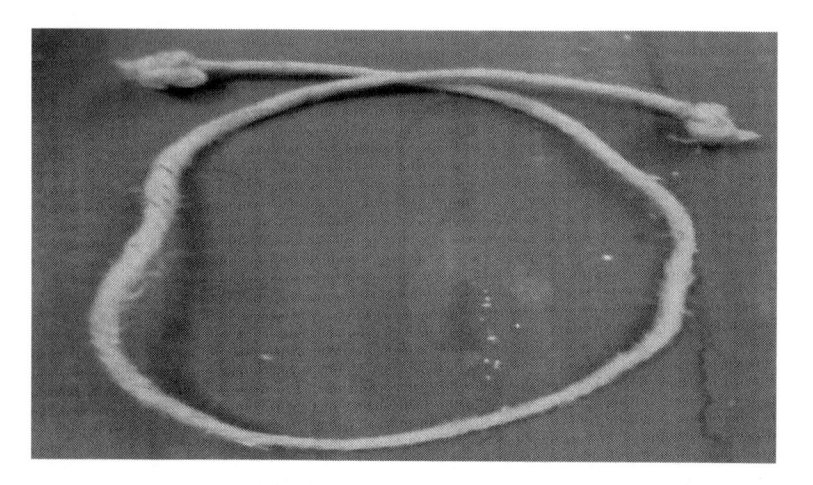

Using the second strand of hemp that you cut (or scrap piece), tie a knot around the ends that are atop one another.

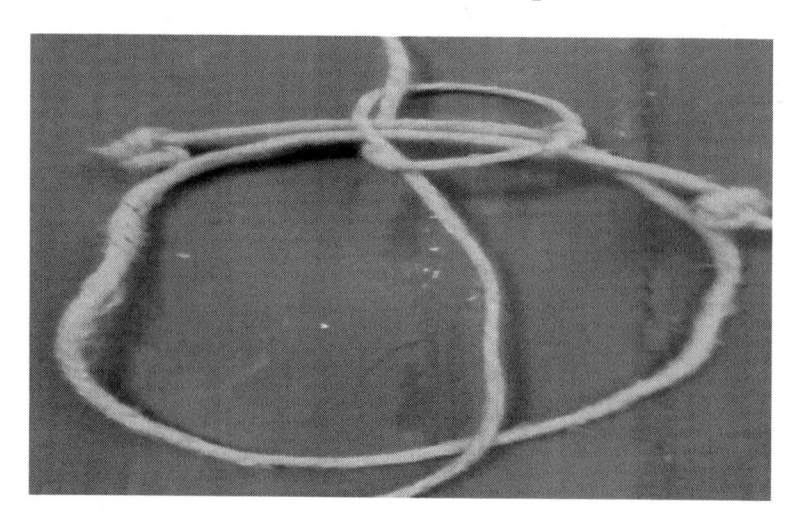

Tie several square knots using this second strand. In this example I have used six square knots. You can use as many or as few as you like to suit your jewelry.

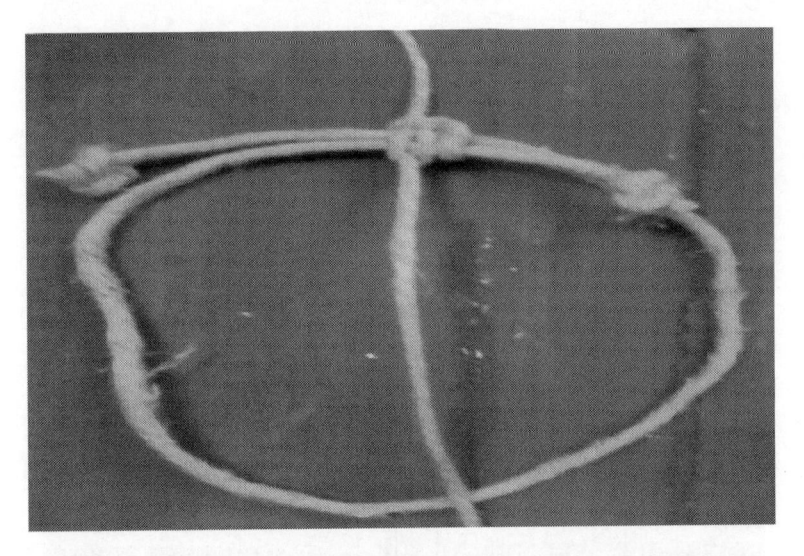

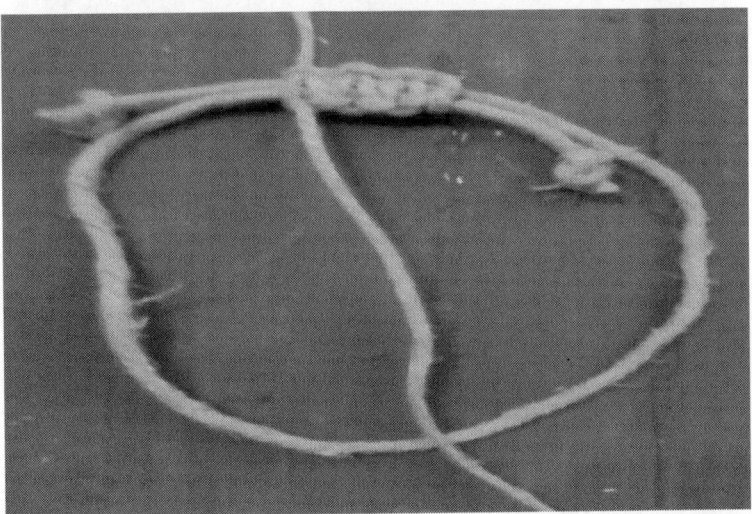

There are a couple of options for ending this closure. Option one is that you can tie an overhand knot at each side of your last square knot. It does provide a little more stability for your closure. However, it may look a little more bulky. Secure with fabric glue.

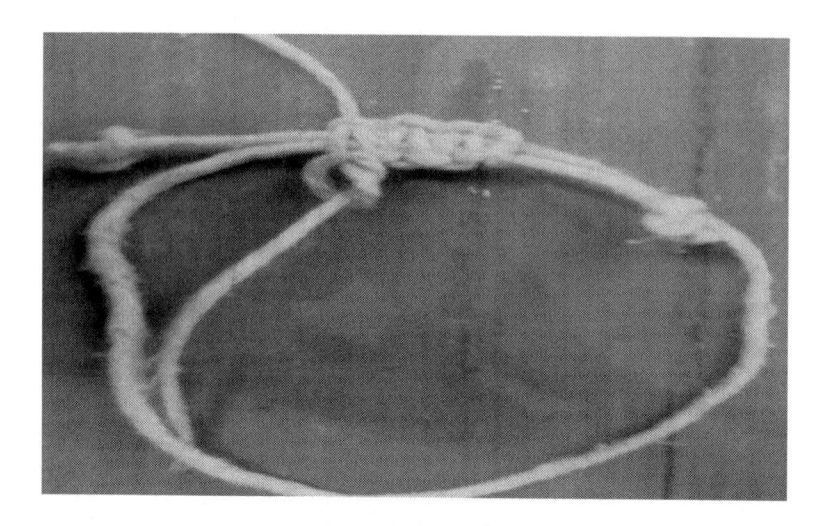

The other option is that you can snip your strands right after your last square knot. It is a little neater looking, but be careful not to snip too close to your knot. Secure with fabric glue.

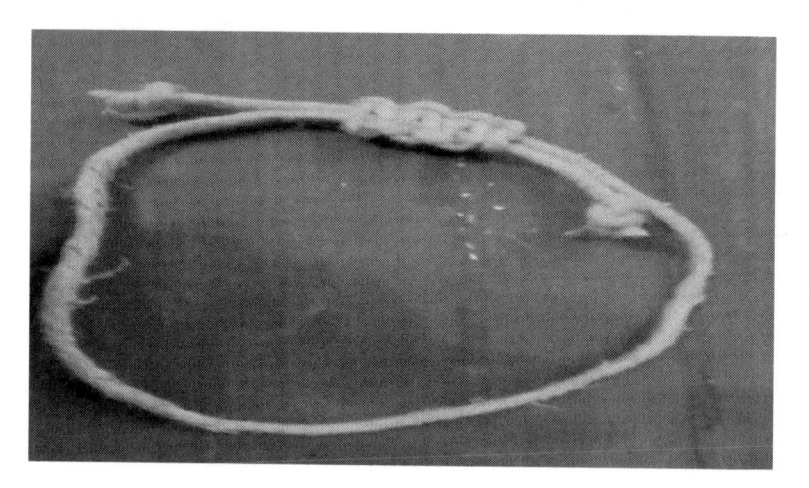

Be careful to only glue the end of your square knot. You might opt to apply your glue with a toothpick or q-tip so that you do not get any on your other strands, as it may prevent them from being able to slide through the closure properly.

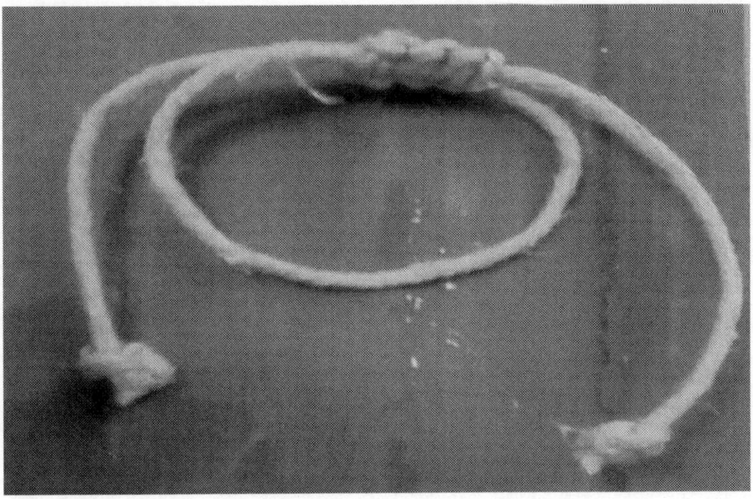

Single Bead Closure

This is an extremely simple closure. This closure could be used to make a double bracelet or anklet if you so desire. In this example I am using one strand.

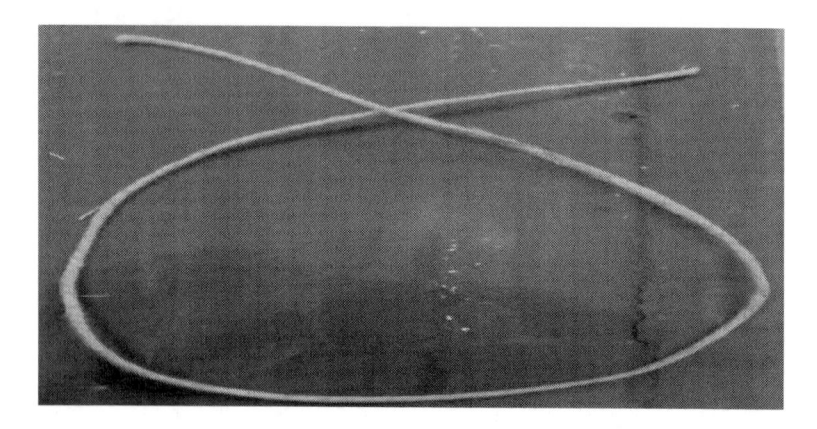

Thread each end of your strand through one bead with the ends of you strand facing opposite directions.

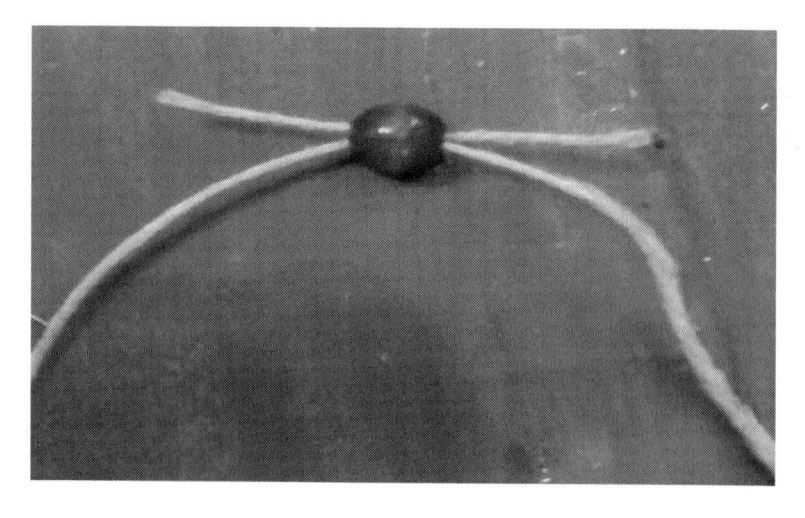

Tie a couple of regular knots around the bead with the ends of your strand.

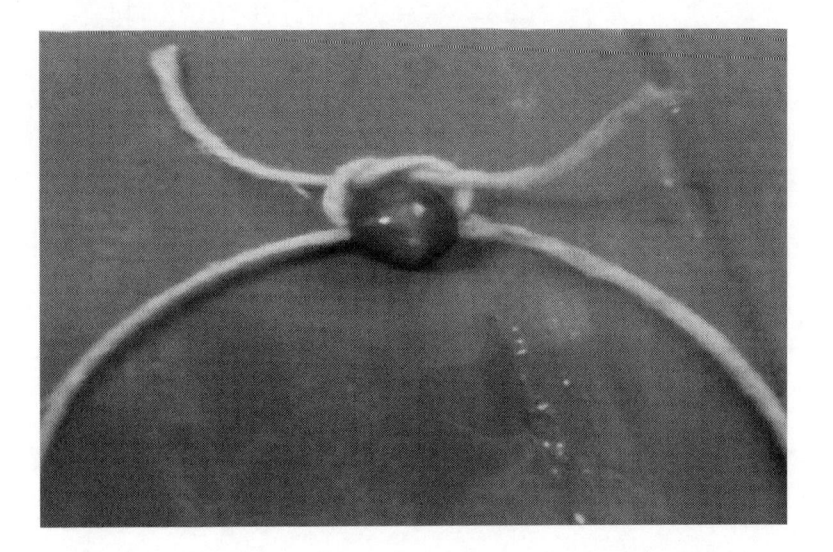

Snip away excess material and secure your knots with fabric glue. Try not to get glue on the bead or other parts of the strand.

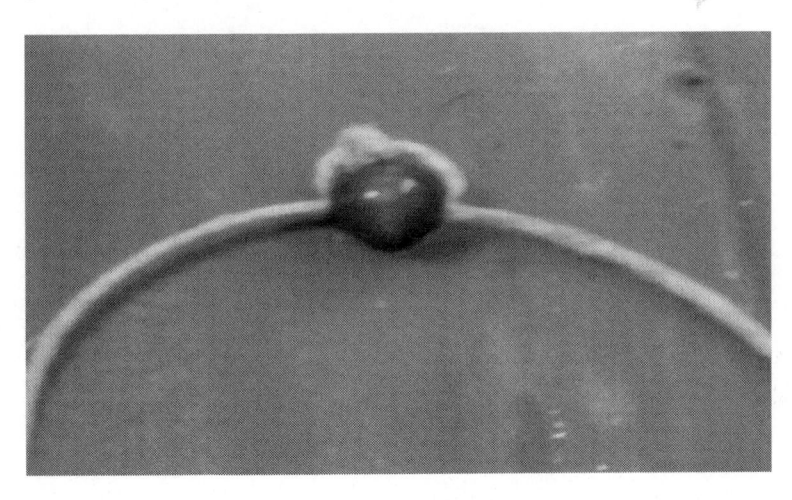

After the glue has dried, grasp the knot between your fingers and pull gently on the bead.

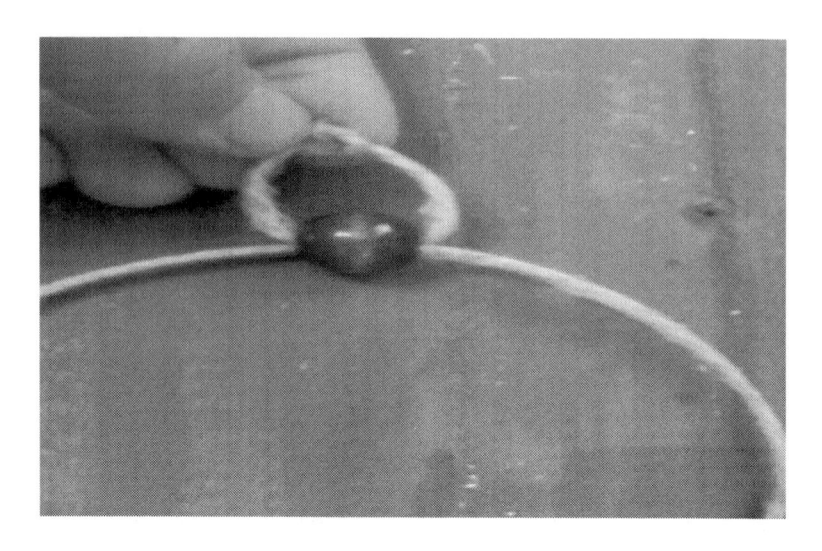

That's it! You have an adjustable piece of jewelry. Just grasp the other end and pull your bead gently back toward your knot to readjust.

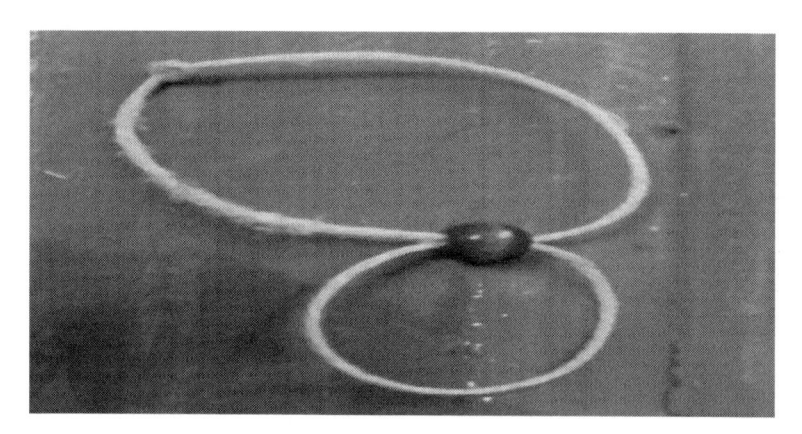

The Butterfly Knot

This is an extremely easy way to make a closure for your jewelry. The butterfly knot works best as a closure when you have begun your jewelry with a loop. The butterfly knot is just a series of square knots and gaps. You will want to leave a bit of room at the end of your jewelry piece to do this. For this example I am using three strands. Typically you would find this knot toward the end of a finished piece, but you can make an entire butterfly knot jewelry piece if you would like. The one shown is only for an example.

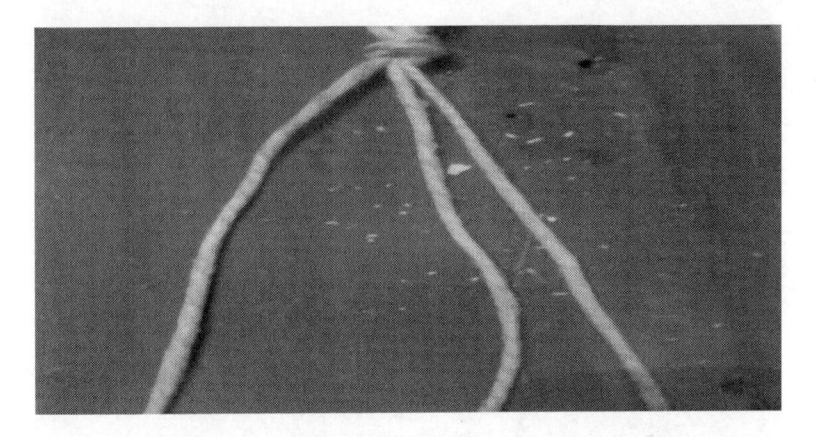

Using the two outer strands, tie a square knot around the middle strand, as shown in the picture below.

Leave a gap and tie another square knot. You should now have a circle, a bit like the circular design in the fishbone.

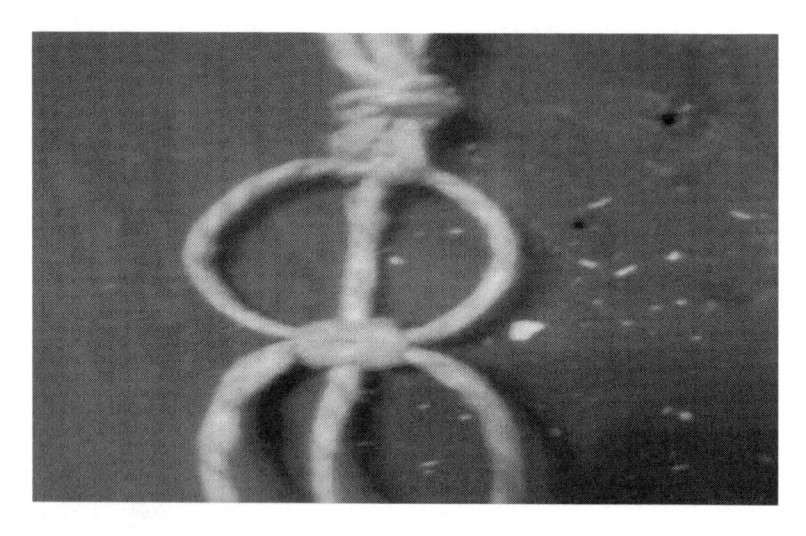

Leave another gap that is about the same size as the first. Tie another square knot, as shown below. Try to keep your circles similar in size.

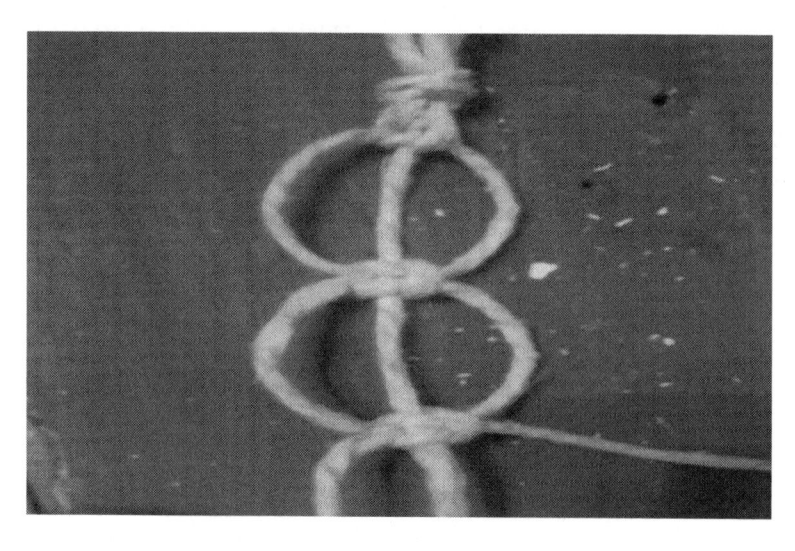

You can slide the square knots up on the middle strand, as shown below.

You can see why this knot is called the butterfly knot. Trim any excess cord from the end of your last square knot. Secure the cut end of your square knot with fabric glue, but be sure not to get any glue on the middle strand. Use the middle strand to tie into the loop at the beginning of the jewelry.

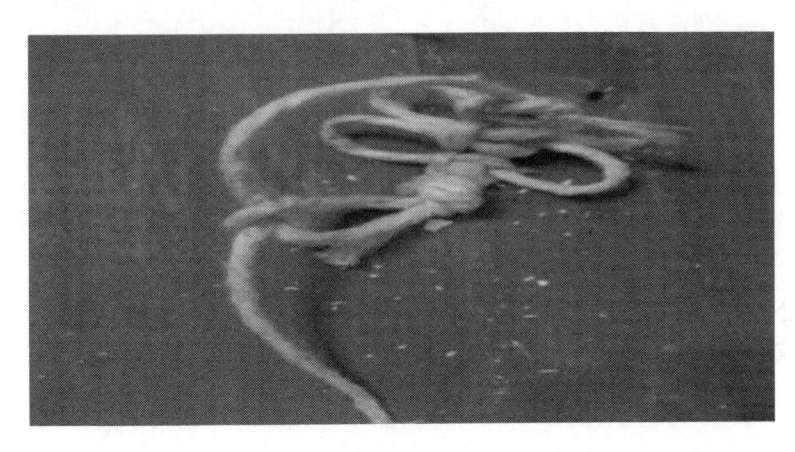

2nd *Single Bead Closure*

The single bead closure is probably the easiest of all of the closures to make. When you are closing your jewelry in this way, you do not want to use a loop in the beginning of your piece. In this example, I am only using one strand. In the picture below, I have tied two overhand knots to represent the ending of a piece of jewelry.

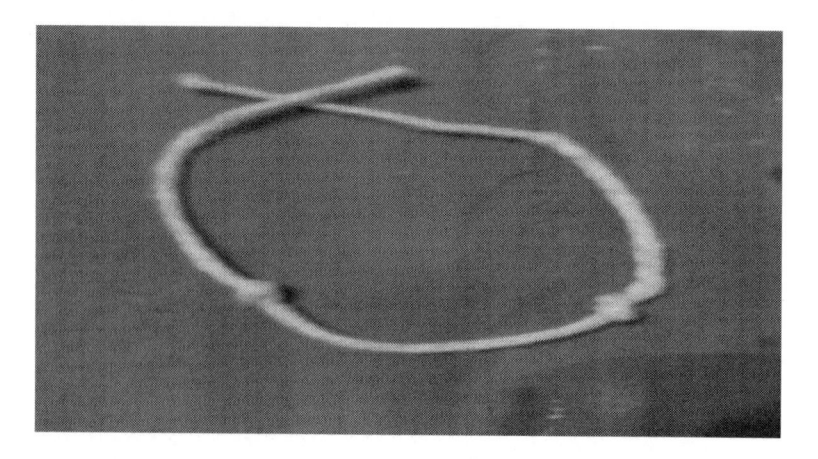

String a bead over both ends of the jewelry, as shown below.

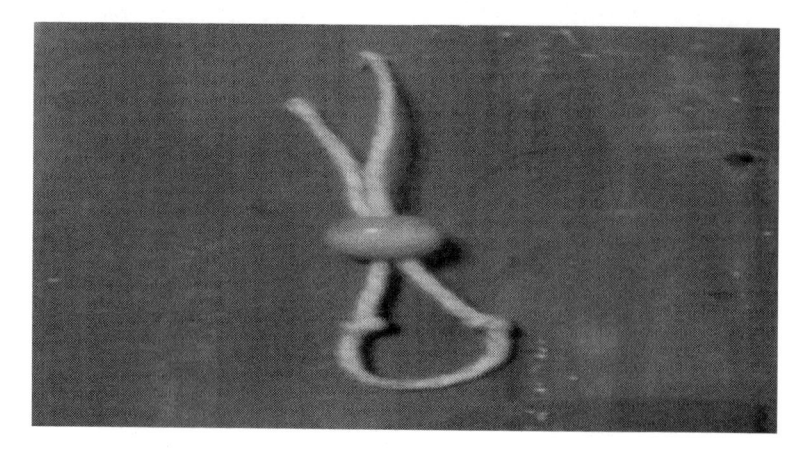

Tie an overhand knot onto each of your strands to keep the bead from sliding off. You could add beads to the end of either strand as well, if you would like. Secure your overhand knots with fabric glue.

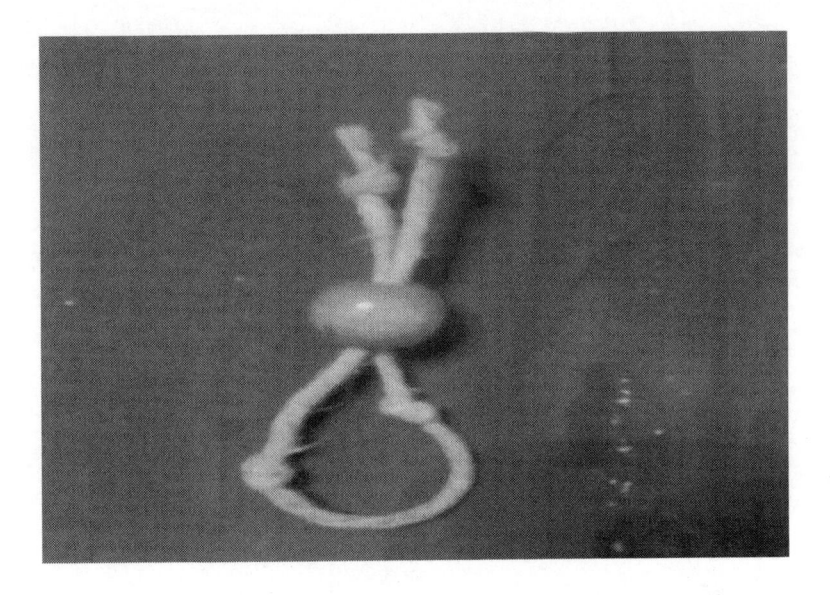

Your bead will slide up and down on your strands, making your jewelry adjustable. Easy as pie!

Multiple Knot Closure

Begin your jewelry with a loop. Leave enough room at the end of your jewelry to tie several overhand knots. The person wearing the jewelry can choose which knot to slide the loop onto. For a more creative edge, you could also add beads to the individual strands between knots.

Multiple Bead Closure

This method is pretty much the same as the multiple knot closure. You should leave enough room at the end of your jewelry to add several beads. Tie overhand knots before and after the beads to secure them. Make sure that the beads are the right size to fit into your loop. The person wearing the jewelry can decide what bead to slip the loop over.

Chapter Review

- Pendants are a great way to add style to your jewelry, and open up more creative options to explore.
- There are variations for any style you choose to make. Create your own variation on a style to personalize your jewelry.
- The closure of your jewelry piece is just as important as the rest of the piece. Go wild. Add beads, colors, whatever you like.
- Mix and match your beads. You are not limited to any one style. This is your art.

To suit a larger variety of people and for a more professional appearance, make your jewelry adjustable.

A Note from the Author

I hope that you have enjoyed reading this guide as much as I have enjoyed making it. For years, jewelry making has been one of my passions and favorite pastimes. I am delighted to be able to share my knowledge with you. I have learned a lot through trial and error, and I continue to learn every day. Don't worry about getting knots or the technique perfect the first time. There is no better way to learn than through a series of mistakes. To quote Thomas Edison: "I didn't fail. I learned 2000 ways not to make a light bulb." I try to keep this quote in mind as I go through life, because it is so easy to just give up.

Though jewelry making takes patience and practice, the results are extremely rewarding. Once you have mastered the basic knots and techniques presented in this guide, you will have opened up thousands of innovative possibilities. The sky is the limit. Personally, I have found countless benefits from learning how to make my own jewelry.

One major benefit is that I save a lot of money by not going out and buying very much jewelry. I also make it as gifts for family and friends for birthdays, special occasions, and holidays. I find that it is much more personal to give something that I have spent time on rather than to go and buy a gift that I have not put very much thought into.

Another benefit is that I can sport jewelry and accessories that are completely unique to my wardrobe. They fit me perfectly and cater to my own personal style. I have yet to buy anything from a department or chain store that suits me quite as well, and I do not think I ever will. It is intensely satisfying to know that what I am wearing is my own artistic creation.

Children and teens love to make hemp jewelry too. Putting together a macramé party for the kids is a lot of fun. For the older kids, making the knots and showing their jewelry off to friends and family feels like quite an accomplishment and may inspire a little healthy competitive edge. Indeed it is an accomplishment. There are few things more satisfying than being able to craft something beautiful and share it with loved ones. Give younger children strands and beads and watch their imagination soar, even if they cannot make the knots. You will be amazed at what they are able to come up with. Not to mention that you are setting the stage for creativity in the future.

Please be aware that beads and hemp cord can be hazardous in the hands and mouth of a toddler, so if you do have toddlers at your party, keep a close eye on them.

Don't skimp on the fun for adults. The adults can be as involved with the hemp jewelry making as the children, or even have an adult macramé party for themselves. Even if you do not have children, a macramé party is a great excuse for getting friends and family together for a night of fun and inventive challenges.

As I said before, the sky is the limit. You do not have to stop at jewelry. Why not go further? You can make tapestries, beaded curtains, shoes, clothing, accessories, bags, furniture coverings, and the list goes on and on. Also, because the price of hemp is so low, you can make a lot of stuff for very little money. This is certainly a craft for the frugal hearted bargain shopper, and for the eco minded as well.

Once you begin making hemp jewelry, you will no doubt be addicted. Whether you are a novice or an expert crafter, there is always something new to learn. New challenges can only make you grow as a crafter and artist.

Thank you for reading this guide. I hope that you have found the information both helpful and interesting. Happy hemping!

About the Expert

Tabitha Clark was born in LaGrange, GA. As a preteen, she moved to the Carrollton, GA area and has been settled there since. Now married with one son, she is a fulltime homemaker, homeschooler and artist. She enjoys painting, writing, photography and cooking, or almost anything that obliges a creative flair.

In her spare time, Tabitha focuses her energy on jewelry making. She has been making and selling hemp jewelry for about ten years and continually experiments with new knots, designs, and beads to craft unique, one of a kind pieces. She is passionate about creating and welcomes every opportunity to share her art and techniques with the world.

HowExpert publishes quick 'how to' guides on all topics from A to Z by everyday experts. Visit HowExpert.com to learn more.

Recommended Resources

- HowExpert.com – Quick 'How To' Guides on All Topics from A to Z by Everyday Experts.
- HowExpert.com/free – Free HowExpert Email Newsletter.
- HowExpert.com/books – HowExpert Books
- HowExpert.com/courses – HowExpert Courses
- HowExpert.com/clothing – HowExpert Clothing
- HowExpert.com/membership – HowExpert Membership Site
- HowExpert.com/affiliates – HowExpert Affiliate Program
- HowExpert.com/writers – Write About Your #1 Passion/Knowledge/Expertise & Become a HowExpert Author.
- HowExpert.com/resources – Additional HowExpert Recommended Resources
- YouTube.com/HowExpert – Subscribe to HowExpert YouTube.
- Instagram.com/HowExpert – Follow HowExpert on Instagram.
- Facebook.com/HowExpert – Follow HowExpert on Facebook.

Made in the USA
Middletown, DE
07 February 2023